THE VISUAL DICTIONARY

UPDATED AND EXPANDED

Written by Simon Beecroft and Jason Fry

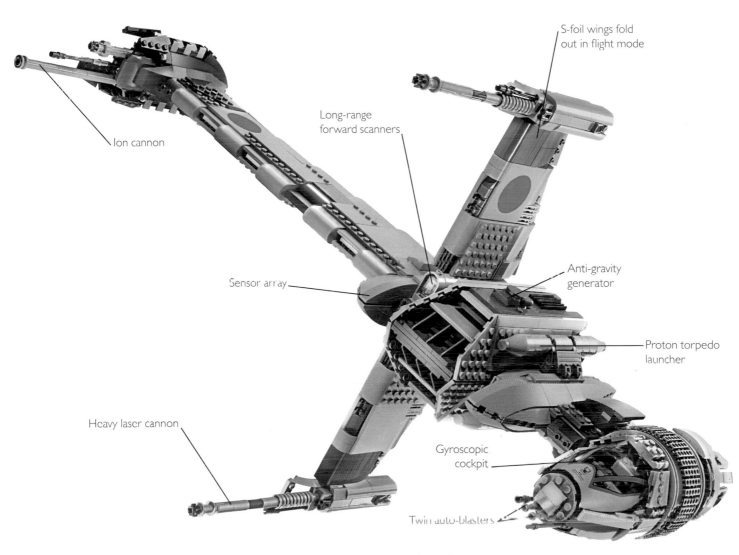

S-foil wings fold out in flight mode

Ion cannon

Long-range forward scanners

Sensor array

Anti-gravity generator

Proton torpedo launcher

Heavy laser cannon

Gyroscopic cockpit

Twin auto-blasters

B-WING STARFIGHTER (2012)

Contents

CHAPTER 3: SPECIALIST SETS

CHAPTER 4: BEYOND THE BRICK

Much to learn, you still have.

Introduction

If *Star Wars* is an extraordinarily rich and detailed fantasy world, LEGO® *Star Wars*® is that same fantasy world made entirely of colored bricks. In LEGO *Star Wars*, the characters, vehicles, settings, and weapons of the movies are instantly recognizable, yet subtly different. A wealth of movie-accurate details surprise and delight even the most dedicated *Star Wars* fans, from the steering vanes on a Tatooine skiff to the chin guns adorning the head of a lumbering AT-AT walker. The LEGO Group's designers are endlessly creative with their lexicon of LEGO elements—such as a cupcake and a smear of frosting given new life as the glowing eye and armored shell of

a droideka. The only thing more enjoyable is encountering new elements made especially for a LEGO *Star Wars* set, such as the printed flap on the cockpit of the mini AT-ST, or a brick from an X-wing cockpit complete with miniature screens and dials. It's as much fun to spot the differences between the movie originals and the LEGO versions, whether it's a change of color, a reconfigured interior, or a new feature. With LEGO *Star Wars*, curiosity is rewarded: Headlamps flip aside to reveal missile launchers, secret compartments hide Holocrons, and Gungan subs sprout their own mini-subs in times of trouble. Originally published in 2009, *LEGO Star Wars: The*

Breath mask

Customized battle armor

Sith lightsaber

SITH WARRIOR

Toothy grin

Ammo bandolier

Multicolored hair

CHEWBACCA

Visual Dictionary has now been thoroughly updated and expanded with five additional years of LEGO designs—yellow faces have become flesh-colored, starfighters and vehicles have been revised with even more detail and movie accuracy, and new *Star Wars* characters and sets have been translated into brick form. Whether a set is brand-new or an established classic, the reason for its appeal has stayed the same: LEGO *Star Wars* exists in both the *Star Wars* world and the LEGO world, making it fascinating to children and collectors alike.

TIMELINE
The LEGO Group released its first *Star Wars* sets in 1999 to coincide with the release of *Star Wars*: Episode I *The Phantom Menace*. Models were then issued for each new movie in the Prequel Trilogy (Episodes I–III), as well as sets based on the Classic Trilogy, the *Star Wars: The Clone Wars* animated TV show, and the computer games *Star Wars: The Force Unleashed* and *Star Wars: The Old Republic*. Then, in 2013, LEGO *Star Wars* developed a new life of its own with the animated TV show *LEGO Star Wars: The Yoda Chronicles*.

DATA BOXES
Throughout the book, each LEGO *Star Wars* set is identified with a data box (see example below), providing the official name of the set, the year it was first released, the LEGO identification number of the set, the number of LEGO pieces, or elements, in the set (excluding minifigures), and the source that inspired the model. The abbreviations "EP I" to "EP VI" are used for each of the six movies (EP I, for instance, being *Star Wars*: Episode I *The Phantom Menace*); "CW" is the animated *Star Wars: The Clone Wars* TV show and movie; and "EU" refers to the Expanded Universe.

Set name	Tusken Raider Encounter	
Year	2002	Number 7113
Pieces	90	Source EP II

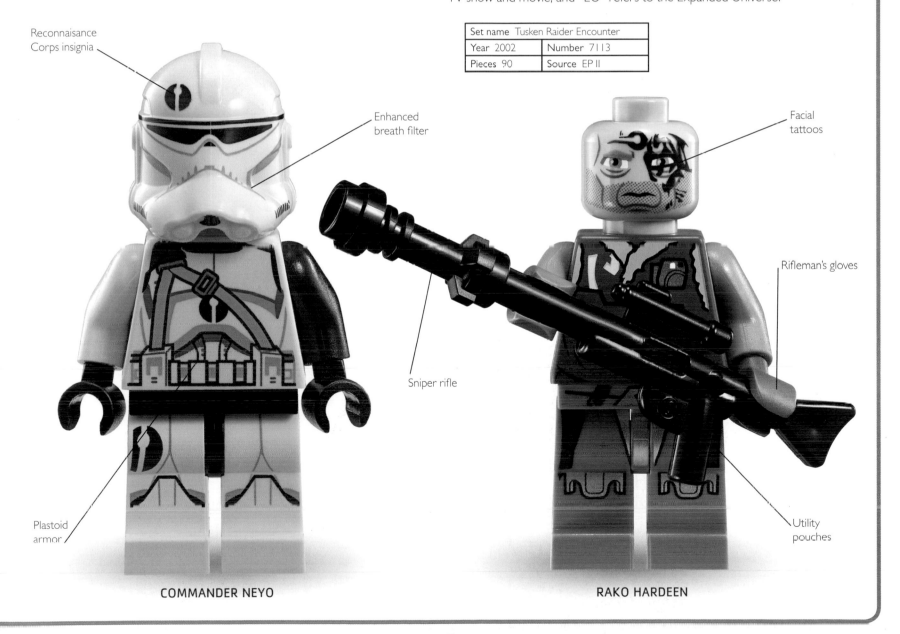

Reconnaisance Corps insignia

Enhanced breath filter

Sniper rifle

Plastoid armor

COMMANDER NEYO

Facial tattoos

Rifleman's gloves

Utility pouches

RAKO HARDEEN

1999

2000

Episode I

7101 Lightsaber Duel ▶

◀ 7111 Droid Fighter

7121 Naboo Swamp ▶

◀ 7131 Anakin's Podracer

7141 Naboo Fighter ▶

◀ 7151 Sith Infiltrator

7161 Gungan Sub ▶

◀ 7171 Mos Espa Podrace

 ◀ 3343 *Star Wars* #4

7115 Gungan Patrol ▶

◀ 7124 Flash Speeder

7155 Trade Federation AAT ▶

◀ 7159 *Star Wars* Bucket

7184 Trade Federation MTT ▶

◀ 8000 Technic Pit Droid

8001 Technic Battle Droid ▶

◀ 8002 Technic Destroyer Droid

LEGO® MINDSTORMS®

9748 Droid Developer Kit ▶

9754 Dark Side Developer Kit ▶

Episode IV

7150 TIE Fighter & Y-Wing ▶

◀ 7110 Landspeeder

7140 X-Wing Fighter ▶

◀ 7190 *Millennium Falcon*

7191 Ultimate Collector Series X-Wing Fighter ▶

 ◀ 3340 *Star Wars* #1

7144 *Slave I* ▶

Episode V

7130 Snowspeeder ▶

 ◀ 3341 *Star Wars* #2

3342 *Star Wars* #3 ▶

Episode VI

7128 Speeder Bikes ▶

 ◀ 7104 Desert Skiff

7134 A-Wing ▶ Fighter

◀ 7181 Ultimate Collector Series TIE Interceptor

7180 B-Wing at Rebel Control Center ▶

2001

7126 Battle Droid Carrier

7186 Watto's Junkyard

10018 Darth Maul

8007 Technic C-3PO

7106 Droid Escape

7146 TIE Fighter

10019 Rebel Blockade Runner

8008 Technic Stormtrooper

7166 Imperial Shuttle

7127 Imperial AT-ST

2002

7203 Jedi Defense I

7204 Jedi Defense II

10026 Ultimate Collector Series Naboo Starfighter

Episode II

7103 Jedi Duel

7113 Tusken Raider Encounter

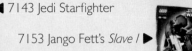

7133 Bounty Hunter Pursuit

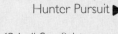

7143 Jedi Starfighter

7153 Jango Fett's *Slave I*

7163 Republic Gunship

8009 Technic R2-D2

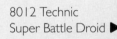

8011 Technic Jango Fett

8012 Technic Super Battle Droid

7142 X-Wing Fighter

7152 TIE Fighter & Y-Wing

3219 Mini TIE Fighter

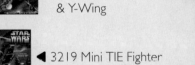

8010 Technic Darth Vader

10030 Ultimate Collector Series Imperial Star Destroyer

7194 Ultimate Collector Series Yoda

7119 Twin-Pod Cloud Car

7139 Ewok Attack

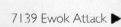

7200 Final Duel I

7201 Final Duel II

2003

4485 Mini Sebulba's Podracer & Anakin's Podracer

4491 Mini MTT

4478 Geonosian Fighter

4481 Hailfire Droid

4482 AT-TE

4490 Mini Republic Gunship

4487 Mini Jedi Starfighter & *Slave I*

4477 T-16 Skyhopper

4484 Mini X-Wing Fighter & TIE Advanced

4488 Mini *Millennium Falcon*

4479 TIE Bomber

4483 AT-AT

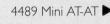

4486 Mini AT-ST & Snowspeeder

4489 Mini AT-AT

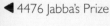

10123 Cloud City

4475 Jabba's Message

4476 Jabba's Prize

4480 Jabba's Palace

4494 Mini Imperial Shuttle

Episode I

4493 Mini Sith ▶
Infiltrator

Episode II

4495 Mini AT-TE ▶

Episode IV

4501 Mos Eisley Cantina ▶

7262 TIE Fighter & Y-Wing ▶

◀10131 TIE Fighter
Collection

10134 Y-Wing ▶
Attack Starfighter

◀ 4492 Mini Star
Destroyer

6963 Mini X-Wing ▶
Fighter

Episode V

◀ 6964 Mini Boba Fett's *Slave I*

4500 Rebel ▶
Snowspeeder

◀ 4502 X-Wing Fighter

10129 Rebel ▶
Snowspeeder

◀ 4504 *Millennium Falcon*

Episode VI

6965 Mini TIE Interceptor ▶

4494 Mini Imperial ▶
Shuttle

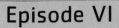
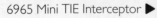

Episode III

6966 Mini Jedi Starfighter ◀

6967 Mini ARC Fighter ▶

◀ 7250 Clone Scout Walker

7251 Darth Vader Transformation ▶

◀ 7252 Droid Tri-Fighter

7255 General Grievous Chase ▶

◀ 7256 Jedi Starfighter & Vulture Droid

7257 Ultimate Lightsaber Duel ▶

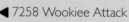

◀ 7258 Wookiee Attack

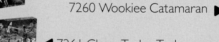

◀ 7259 ARC-170 Starfighter

7260 Wookiee Catamaran ▶

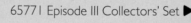

◀ 7261 Clone Turbo Tank

◀7283 Ultimate Space Battle

65771 Episode III Collectors' Set ▶

◀ 7263 TIE Fighter

10144 Sandcrawler ▶

◀ 7264 Imperial
Inspection

10143 Death Star II ▶

 6205 V-Wing Fighter

6211 Imperial Star Destroyer ▶

 ◀ 10175 Vader's TIE Advanced

6212 X-Wing Fighter ▶

 6209 *Slave I* ▶

6206 TIE Interceptor ▶

6207 A-Wing Fighter ◀

6208 B-Wing Fighter ▶

 ◀ 6210 Jabba's Sail Barge

 10174 Ultimate Collector's Imperial AT-ST ▶

7660 Naboo N-1 Starfighter and Vulture Droid ▶

 ◀ 7662 Trade Federation MTT

 ◀ 7663 Sith Infiltrator

7665 Republic Cruiser ▶

 ◀ 7656 General Grievous Starfighter

7661 Jedi Starfighter with Hyperdrive Booster Ring ▶

7654 Droids Battle Pack ▶

7655 Clone Troopers Battle Pack ▶

 ◀ 7658 Y-Wing Fighter

7659 Imperial Landing Craft ▶

 10179 Ultimate Collector's *Millennium Falcon*

 ◀ 7666 Hoth Rebel Base

10178 Motorized Walking AT-AT ▶

◀ 7657 AT-ST

Expanded Universe

7661 TIE Crawler ▶

Episode I

Episode II

7670 Hailfire Droid ▶
& Spider Droid

 7778 Midi-scale *Millennium Falcon* ▶

◀ 10198 *Tantive IV*

Episode III

 ◀ 7671 AT-AP
Walker

10186 General ▶
Grievous

8017 Darth
Vader's TIE Fighter ▶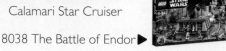

7749 Echo Base ▶

 ◀ 20006 Mini Clone Turbo Tank

 ◀ 7754 *Home One* Mon
Calamari Star Cruiser

8038 The Battle of Endor ▶

Episode IV

10188 Death Star ▶

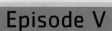 ◀ 8028 Mini TIE Fighter

30005 Mini Imperial Speeder Bike ▶

30004 Mini Battle Droid on STAP ▶

Episode V

 ◀ 8029 Mini Rebel
Snowspeeder

◀ 30006 Mini Clone Walker

20009 Mini AT-TE ▶

Episode VI

 ◀ 20010 Mini Republic Gunship

7748 Corporate Alliance ▶
Tank Droid

Expanded Universe

7668 Rebel Scout Speeder ▶

 ◀ 7751 Ahsoka's Starfighter
and Vulture Droids

 ◀ 7667 Imperial Dropship

7672 *Rogue Shadow* ▶

7752 Count Dooku's ▶
Solar Sailer

 ◀ 7753 Pirate Tank

Clone Wars

 7669 Anakin's Jedi Starfighter ▶

8014 Clone Walker Battle Pack ▶

◀ 7670 Hailfire Droid & Spider Droid

 ◀ 8015 Assassin Droids Battle Pack

7673 Magna Guard Starfighter ▶

8016 Hyena Droid Bomber ▶

 ◀ 7674 V-19 Torrent

 ◀ 8018 AAT

7675 AT-TE Walker ▶

8019 Republic Attack Shuttle ▶

 ◀ 7676 Republic Attack Gunship

 ◀ 8036 Separatist Shuttle

7678 Droid Gunship ▶

8037 Anakin's Y-Wing ▶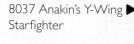
Starfighter

 ◀ 7679 Republic
Fighter Tank

7680 The *Twilight* ▶

 ◀ 8033 Mini General Grievous Starfighter

◀ 7681 Separatist Spider Droid

8039 *Venator*-Class Republic ▶
Attack Cruiser

8031 Mini V-19 Torrent ▶

 ◀ 20007 Mini Republic Attack Cruiser

 ◀ 10195 Republic Dropship with AT-OT

10215 Obi-Wan's Jedi Starfighter ▶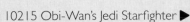

 ◀ 8091 Republic Swamp Speeder
8096 Emperor Palpatine's Shuttle ▶

 8092 Luke's Landspeeder
8099 Midi-scale Imperial ▶
Star Destroyer

◀ 8083 Rebel Trooper Battle Pack

8084 Snowtrooper Battle Pack ▶

 ◀ 8089 Hoth Wampa Cave

8097 Slave I ▶

 ◀ 8129 AT-AT Walker

30051 X-Wing Fighter ▶

 ◀ 20018 AT-AT Walker

 ◀ 20016 Imperial Shuttle
10212 Imperial Shuttle ▶

 ◀ 8087 TIE Defender

 ◀ 8085 Freeco Speeder
8086 Droid Tri-Fighter ▶

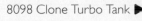 ◀ 8088 ARC-170 Starfighter
8093 Plo Koon's Jedi Starfighter ▶

 ◀ 8095 General Grievous Starfighter
8098 Clone Turbo Tank ▶

 ◀ 8128 Cad Bane's Speeder
30050 Republic Attack Shuttle ▶

7877 Naboo Starfighter ▶
 ◀ 7929 The Battle Of Naboo

7961 Darth Maul's Sith Infiltrator ▶
 ◀ 7962 Anakin's & Sebulba's Podracer

30052 Mini AAT ▶
 ◀ 30055 Mini Vulture Droid

30053 Mini Republic Attack Cruiser ▶

 ◀ 7965 Millennium Falcon

10221 Ultimate
Collector Series
Super Star
Destroyer ▶  7879 Hoth ▶ Echo Base
▲ 20019 Mini Slave I

7956 Ewok Attack ▶  ◀ 30054 Mini AT-ST

 ◀ 7958 Advent Calendar
7915 Imperial V-Wing Starfighter ▶

7868 Mace Windu's Jedi Starfighter ▶
 ◀ 7869 Battle For Geonosis

7913 Clone Trooper Battle Pack ▶

 ◀ 7914 Mandalorian Battle Pack

20021 Mini Bounty Hunter ▶
Assault Gunship

 ◀ 7930 Bounty Hunter Assault Gunship

7931 T-6 Jedi Shuttle ▶

 ◀ 7957 Sith Nightspeeder

7959 Geonosian Starfighter ▶
◀ 7964 Republic Frigate

 **2012**

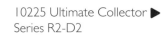 **2013**

Episode I

◀ 9674 Planet Set: Naboo Starfighter & Naboo

◀ 9675 Planet Set: Sebulba's Podracer & Tatooine

9499 Gungan Sub ▶

 10225 Ultimate Collector Series R2-D2 ▶

◀ 30057 Mini Anakin's Podracer

◀ 30059 Mini MTT

30058 Mini STAP ▶

Episode II

75000 Clone Troopers vs Droidekas ▶

 ◀ 75006 Jedi Starfighter & Kamino

75015 Corporate Alliance Tank Droid ▶

 ◀ 75007 Republic Assault Ship & Coruscant

75011 *Tantive IV* and Alderaan ▶

Episode III

 9494 Anakin's Jedi Interceptor ▶

◀ 9526 Palpatine's Arrest

Episode IV

 ◀ 9490 Droid Escape

9492 TIE Fighter ▶

◀ 9493 X-Wing Starfighter

9495 Gold Leader's Y-Wing Starfighter ▶

◀ 9676 Planet Set: TIE Interceptor & Death Star

◀ 30056 Mini Star Destroyer

9677 Planet Set: X-Wing Starfighter & Yavin 4 ▶

 ◀ 75008 TIE Bomber & Asteroid Field

75009 Snowspeeder & Hoth ▶

Episode V

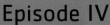 ◀ 3866 LEGO® Games: The Battle of Hoth

9678 Planet Set: Twin-pod Cloud Car & Bespin ▶

10236 Ewok Village ▶

▲ 75003 A-Wing Starfighter

Episode VI

 ◀ 9489 Endor Rebel Trooper & Imperial Battle Pack

◀ 9496 Desert Skiff ▶

◀ 9516 Jabba's Palace

9679 Planet Set: AT-ST & Endor ▶

▲ 10227 B-Wing Starfighter

◀ 75001 Republic Troopers vs Sith Troopers

75018 JEK-14's Stealth Starfighter ▶

Expanded Universe

 ◀ 9500 Sith *Fury* Class Interceptor

9509 Advent ▶ Calendar

9497 Republic *Striker*-class Starfighter ▶

◀ 75002 AT-RT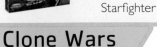

75004 Z-95 Headhunter ▶

Clone Wars

 ◀ 9488 Elite Clone Trooper & Commando Droid Battle Pack

9491 Geonosian Cannon ▶

◀ 9498 Saesee Tiin's Jedi Starfighter ▶

◀ 9515 The Malevolence

9525 Pre Vizsla's Mandalorian Fighter ▶

◀ 75012 BARC Speeder with Sidecar

75013 Umbaran MHC ▶ (Mobile Heavy Cannon)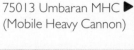

75029 AAT ▶

75016 Homing
Spider Droid ▶

◀ 75017 Duel
on Geonosis

75019 AT-TE ▶

◀ 75021 Republic Gunship

◀ 30244 Anakin's Jedi Interceptor

30247 ARC-170 Starfighter ▶

◀ 75028 Clone Turbo Tank

75035 Kashyyyk Troopers ▶
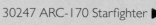

◀ 75036 Utapau Troopers

75037 Battle on Saleucami ▶

◀ 75038 Jedi Interceptor

75040 General
Grievous' Wheel Bike ▶

◀ 75039 V-Wing Starfighter

75041 Vulture Droid ▶

◀ 10240 Red Five
X-wing Starfighter

◀ 75014 Battle of Hoth ▶

◀ 75042 Droid Gunship

75043 AT-AP ▶

◀ 75044 Droid Tri-Fighter

◀ 75030 *Millennium Falcon*

75032 X-Wing Fighter ▶

◀ 75033 Star Destroyer

75034 Death Star Troopers ▶

◀ 75010
B-Wing
Starfighter
and Endor

▲ 75005 Rancor Pit

75020 Jabba's Sail Barge ▶

◀ 75055 Star
Destroyer

◀ 75052 Mos
Eisley Cantina

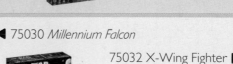

◀ 75023 Advent Calendar

75025 Jedi *Defender-*
Class Cruiser

75054 AT-AT ▶

◀ 75022 Mandalorian
Speeder

75024 HH-87 Starhopper ▶

◀ 75059 Sandcrawler

◀ 30240 Z-95 Headhunter

30241 Mandalorian Fighter ▶

◀ 30246 Imperial
Shuttle

75031 TIE Interceptor ▶

◀ 30212 Republic Frigate

30243 Umbaran MHC ▶

◀ 75045 Republic AV-7
Anti-Vehicle Cannon

75046 Coruscant Police Gunship ▶

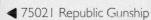

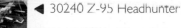

Chapter 1:
Prequel Trilogy
& Clone Wars

Anakin Skywalker

Anakin's journey from a slave boy to perhaps the most capable and ambitious Jedi ever is filled with action and danger. Anakin has always been an incredible pilot and has flown everything from "borrowed" speeders to custom-designed Jedi starfighters during the Clone Wars. But Anakin's daring has its price: The loss of his hand in battle with Count Dooku starts a process of dehumanization that will end in the full body armor of Darth Vader.

Flight helmet with goggles raised

Determined expression

Slave's tunic

Short unposeable legs

ANAKIN (NABOO PILOT)

SET HISTORY

Naboo N-1 Starfighter & Vulture Droid
Year 2007
Number 7660

Naboo Fighter
Year 1999
Number 7141

Anakin's flying helmet can be swapped with hair

Hidden missile launcher

R2-D2

Set name	Naboo Starfighter	
Year	2011	Number 7877
Pieces	318	Source EP I

Ionization chamber

Engine heat sink

Naboo Starfighter

As a boy, Anakin flies a Naboo N-1 starfighter and blows up the Trade Federation's Droid Control Ship. He fits in the cockpit, boarding the fighter via a ladder that extends from the cargo speeder included with this set. A mechanism on the underside ejects R2-D2 from the droid socket in case of trouble. In this set Anakin has a natural face color and short legs. Swiveling his head reveals another face, wearing Podracing goggles.

Coruscant Airspeeder

Teenage Anakin is now a headstrong Padawan, training under Jedi Master Obi-Wan Kenobi. Anakin wears a Padawan braid (printed on his minifigure's shirt.) He and Obi-Wan sit in this airspeeder with its exposed turbojets. The Jedi store their lightsabers in a secret compartment. Can the Jedi catch up with assassin Zam Wesell's speeder, as they weave through the skyscrapers of the city planet, Coruscant?

Speeder features no seats or controls!

Headlights (used as cups in other LEGO sets)

Turbojet engines

Set name	Bounty Hunter Pursuit	
Year	2002	Number 7133
Pieces	253	Source EP II

ANAKIN (PADAWAN)

YOUNG PADAWAN
Protecting Padmé Amidala, Anakin falls in love with the brave senator. He briefly wields a green lightsaber on Geonosis. This figure came with the Republic Gunship (set 75021).

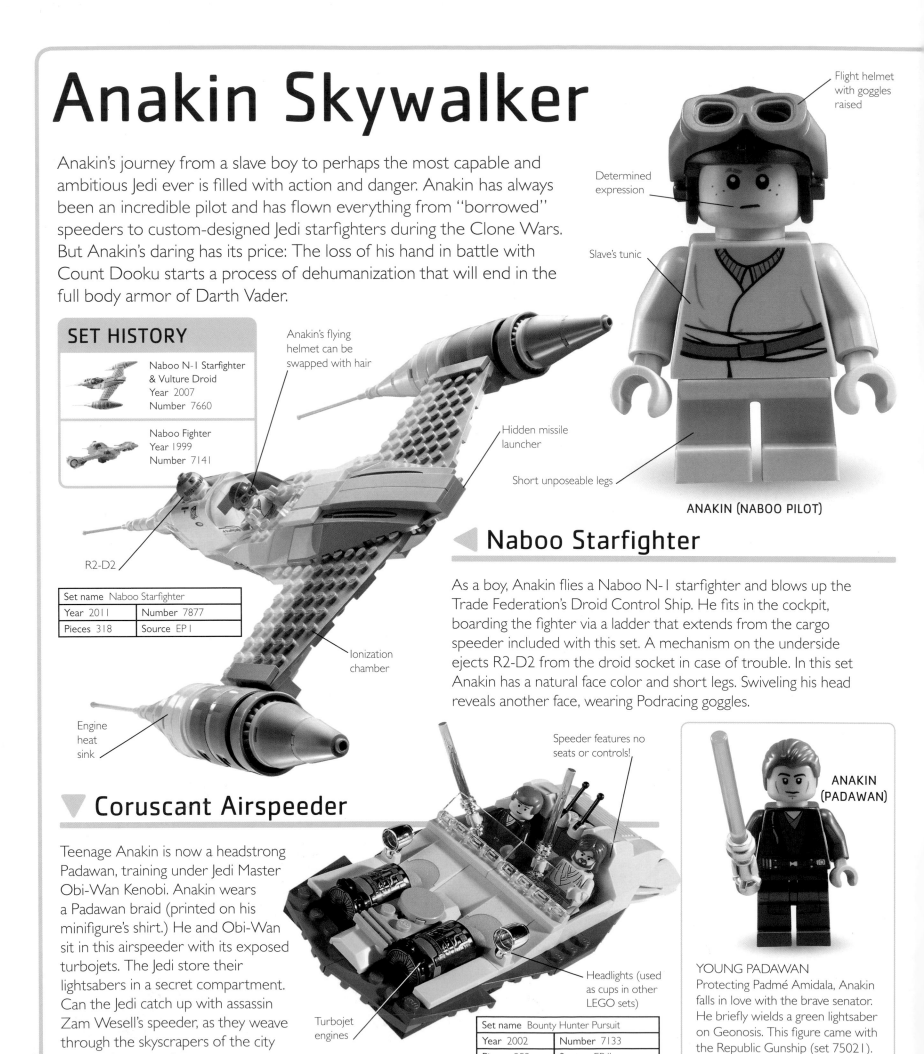

PADMÉ (PEASANT DISGUISE)

UNDERCOVER QUEEN
When Anakin first meets his future wife, Padmé Naberrie is disguised as a peasant for her trip to Tatooine. In Darth Maul's Sith Infiltrator (set 7961), Padmé has a natural skin tone.

▼ Swoop Bike

Padawan Anakin borrows Owen Lars's swoop bike to rescue his mother from the two Tusken Raiders included with this set. The bike has a second seat behind Anakin. Watch out for that moisture vaporator, Anakin! (The vaporator comes with the set and opens to reveal secret controls.)

Jedi cloak

Moisture collection bar

Hinged platform

MOISTURE VAPORATOR

Steering vane

Set name	Tusken Raider Encounter	
Year	2002	Number 7113
Pieces	90	Source EP II

Large viewport

◄ Jedi Starfighter

Anakin is now a Jedi Knight, with a scarred face, pilot headset, cyborg hand, and black robe. He pilots a custom yellow starfighter (actually, an Eta-2 *Actis* Interceptor) with movable wings and R2-D2's accompanying minifigure fully fixed in the astromech socket. The original version in 2005 featured only R2-D2's headpiece.

Hinged radiator wing

Laser cannon

Ion cannon

Republic insignia

SET HISTORY

Jedi Starfighter and Vulture Droid
Year 2005
Number 7256

Set name	Jedi Interceptor	
Year	2014	Number 75038
Pieces	223	Source EP III

JEDI KNIGHT
After a lightsaber duel with Count Dooku, Anakin has a cyborg hand. Turn his head to reveal his Sith eyes after falling to the dark side. This minifigure, complete with brown Jedi cape, came with Palpatine's Arrest (set 9526).

ANAKIN (JEDI/SITH)

Laser turret

Deployable escape pod

► The *Twilight*

Anakin's personal starship in the Clone Wars is a battered Corellian G9 Rigger freighter, the *Twilight*. Anakin first "borrows" the damaged ship from a landing platform on Teth, when he and Ahsoka Tano are rescuing Jabba the Hutt's son, Rotta. Anakin has since repaired and upgraded its weapons and systems.

Ventral cannon

Interior hold includes working two-cable winch

Set name	The *Twilight*	
Year	2008	Number 7680
Pieces	882	Source CW

Podracing

Ladies and gentlemen, Dugs and Hutts, please join us at the Boonta Eve Classic, the most keenly fought and downright dangerous Podrace on Tatooine. Experienced racers Sebulba, Gasgano, and Aldar Beedo will power up their oversized podracers, while the human newcomer, nine-year-old Anakin Skywalker, climbs aboard his self-made machine, watched nervously by his supporters. The tension here is electric!

▼ Starters' Box

The Podrace starts and finishes at the starters' box, with shaded towers for race officials and the press.

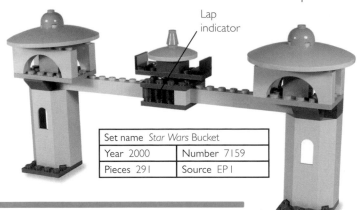

Lap indicator

Set name	*Star Wars* Bucket	
Year	2000	Number 7159
Pieces	291	Source EP1

▶ Sebulba's Podracer

The dastardly Dug named Sebulba is determined to win the Boonta Eve Classic—and doesn't care what dirty tricks he uses to do so. Sebulba's Podracer sports secret flip-up saws that the Dug uses to saw through rival racers' machines, along with opening flaps on the nozzles of his turbocharged engines.

SEBULBA

Afterburner

Control power generator

Combustion chamber

SET HISTORY

Mos Espa Podrace
Year 1999
Number 7171

Set name	Anakin & Sebulba's Podracers	
Year	2011	Number 7962
Pieces	810	Source EP1

▼ Anakin's Podracer

What's that blur on the Tatooine horizon? It's Anakin, in flying goggles, piloting his super-fast podracer with "glowing" power couplings and hinged front air scoops (for additional control when cornering). Anakin built the pod himself, and relies on his Force-aided reflexes while racing. Padmé hopes Anakin will at least survive this dangerous enterprise.

ANAKIN
(PODRACER)

SLAVE SPECTATOR
A Mos Espa slave, the Rodian Wald, cheers on Anakin as he races in the Boonta Eve Classic. But Wald doubts Anakin can win the race—after all, he's never even managed to finish a competition before.

WALD

Throttle lever

Control cable

Set name	Anakin & Sebulba's Podracers	
Year	2011	Number 7962
Pieces	810	Source EP1

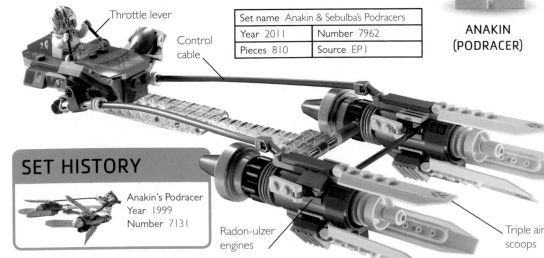

SET HISTORY

Anakin's Podracer
Year 1999
Number 7131

Radon-ulzer engines

Triple air scoops

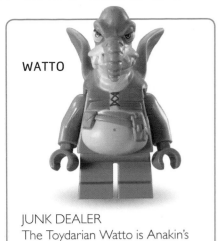

▼ Boonta Eve Podracers

Tatooine podracer pilots such as Gasgano and Aldar Beedo rely on super-fast vehicles to stand a chance of winning the Boonta Eve Classic. Beedo looks for ways to make his Mark IV Flat-Twin Turbojet Podracer even faster, while Gasgano fine-tunes his Ord Pedrovia Podracer. Watto's junkyard is the place to find spare parts and custom accessories, or even to build a new craft. Perhaps parts from Mawhonic's GPE-3130 racer might prove useful—but both racers know that the winged Toydarian drives a hard bargain.

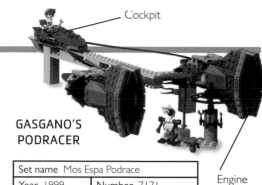

Cockpit

GASGANO'S PODRACER

Engine air intake

Set name Mos Espa Podrace	
Year 1999	Number 7171
Pieces 894	Source EP1

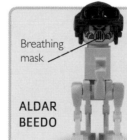

Armored turbojet

MAWHONIC'S PODRACER

Secondary thruster

ALDAR BEEDO'S PODRACER

Set name Watto's Junkyard	
Year 2001	Number 7186
Pieces 466	Source EP1

Flip-up saw

Race decal

Air intake

Energy binder

Repulsor generator housing

Coolant radiators

Split-X stabilizing vane

BRICK FACTS

Breathing mask

ALDAR BEEDO

Aldar Beedo appears in two forms. This version, from the *Star Wars* Bucket (set 7159, from 2000), is made from battle droid pieces: His head has a breathing mask and pilot's helmet. But in Watto's Junkyard (set 7186, from 2001), he has a custom mold.

▼ Other Podracers

Lined up and ready to race, simplified versions of Anakin's and Aldar Beedo's Podracers rev up alongside Neva Kee's experimental machine, with its cockpit placed in front of the massive engines (which could be dangerous!), and Clegg Holdfast's Volvec KT9 Wasp Podracer, with a winged protective canopy over its cockpit.

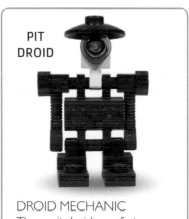

ALDAR BEEDO'S PODRACER

Canopy over command chair

ANAKIN'S PODRACER

NEVA KEE'S PODRACER

CLEGG HOLDFAST'S PODRACER

Set name *Star Wars* Bucket	
Year 2000	Number 7159
Pieces 291	Source EP1

Obi-Wan Kenobi

For a Jedi who's not crazy about flying, Obi-Wan Kenobi pilots a starfighter a lot of the time—though he can't help losing them, too! Kenobi trains headstrong Anakin Skywalker and goes on missions to far-flung planets including Utapau and Mustafar. Under the Empire, an exiled Obi-Wan meets Luke Skywalker and fights a final duel against his former Padawan, now named Darth Vader.

Jedi hood

Utility belt

▲ Padawan

In *Star Wars*: Episode I *The Phantom Menace*, Obi-Wan is Qui-Gon Jinn's Padawan, and joins his master in trying to protect Queen Amidala from the Sith warrior Darth Maul. Obi-Wan is capable but sometimes headstrong—swivel his 2011 head to reveal a face with a knowing smirk that might have led to a stern lecture from Master Qui-Gon.

OBI-WAN (JEDI KNIGHT)

JEDI TEACHER
Anakin proves to be a rebellious apprentice, which may explain Obi-Wan's testy expression here. Previous Episode II minifigures of Obi-Wan had yellow faces. This minifigure is from the Republic Gunship set (75021).

▼ Jedi Starfighter

A yellow-faced Kenobi, Jedi Master to Anakin Skywalker, wears a headset when piloting his Delta-7 *Aethersprite* light interceptor. Kenobi's trusty astromech, R4-P17 (styled slightly differently from the movie), provides support. Together, they duel with Jango Fett's *Slave 1*, blasting by the asteroids above rocky Geonosis!

Deflector shield power hub

Storage area for lightsaber

R4-P17 astromech droid (dome only)

Laser cannon

Communications dish beneath hull

Set name	Jedi Starfighter	
Year	2002	Number 7143
Pieces	138	Source EP II

▼ Jedi Interceptor (Red)

During the battle above Coruscant, Kenobi (now with a flesh-colored face) pilots a red Eta-2 *Actis* Interceptor. This ship is available only in this set, which also includes Anakin's yellow Interceptor, two vulture droids, a tri-fighter, and—watch out, Obi-Wan!—two buzz droids.

R4-P17 dome (restyled)

Buzz droid

Laser cannon

Set name	Ultimate Space Battle	
Year	2005	Number 7283
Pieces	567	Source EP III

▼ Jedi Interceptor (Blue)

After the destruction of his red Eta-2 Interceptor in the Battle of Coruscant, Obi-Wan pilots a blue Interceptor on his mission to Utapau, with a bronze-domed R4-G9 in the astromech socket. Like all Interceptors, this ship is too small to feature a hyperdrive, so it must connect to an external hyperdrive booster ring. Jedi Master Kit Fisto, also included with the set, provides backup.

Set name	Jedi Starfighter with Hyperdrive Booster Ring	
Year	2007	Number 7661
Pieces	575	Source EP III

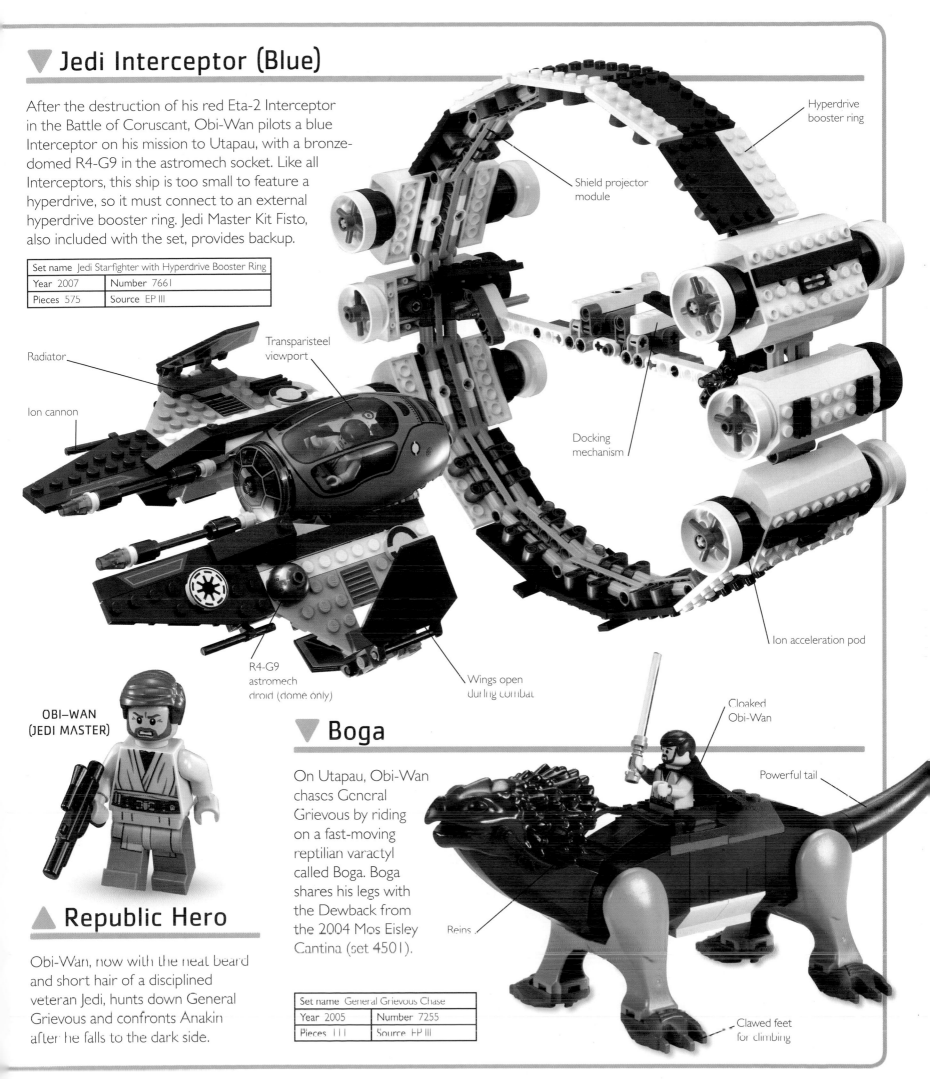

Hyperdrive booster ring

Shield projector module

Docking mechanism

Ion acceleration pod

Radiator

Transparisteel viewport

Ion cannon

R4-G9 astromech droid (dome only)

Wings open during combat

OBI–WAN (JEDI MASTER)

▲ Republic Hero

Obi-Wan, now with the neat beard and short hair of a disciplined veteran Jedi, hunts down General Grievous and confronts Anakin after he falls to the dark side.

▼ Boga

On Utapau, Obi-Wan chases General Grievous by riding on a fast-moving reptilian varactyl called Boga. Boga shares his legs with the Dewback from the 2004 Mos Eisley Cantina (set 4501).

Set name	General Grievous Chase	
Year	2005	Number 7255
Pieces	111	Source EP III

Cloaked Obi-Wan

Powerful tail

Reins

Clawed feet for climbing

Jedi Order

For millennia, the Jedi were the guardians of peace and justice in the galaxy. Within their massive temple on Coruscant, they trained children strong in the Force to become new generations of Padawans, Jedi Knights, and eventually Jedi Masters. During the Clone Wars, the Jedi became military leaders, fighting alongside clone troopers—but in vain. The Sith emerged victorious and destroyed the Jedi ranks as darkness engulfed the galaxy.

Sensitive ears

Green lightsaber blade

Short legs are unhinged

◀ Yoda

Grand Master Yoda helped train Dooku before the Count abandoned the Jedi Order and joined the Sith. This minifigure, with its animation-style eye printing and head mold, looks like it could have jumped off the screen. It's from Duel on Geonosis (set 75017), released in 2013, in which Yoda saves Anakin and Obi-Wan after Dooku defeats them in a saber duel.

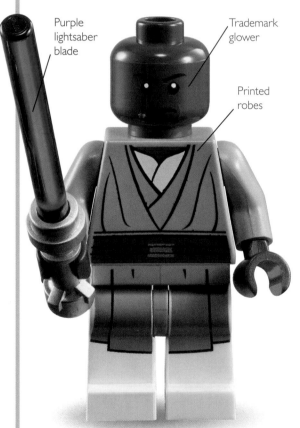

Purple lightsaber blade

Trademark glower

Printed robes

▲ Mace Windu

A member of the Jedi Council, Mace is renowned for his skill with a lightsaber and his stern manner. His minifigure's saber blade is a unique purple. As a senior member of the Council, Mace commands great respect from younger Jedi, who rarely risk his wrath. Other minifigures with "bald" head pieces include Lobot, Asajj Ventress, Sugi, Turk Falso, and the Tusken Raider.

▼ Jedi Masters

A Jedi who has trained a Padawan through to Jedi Knighthood earns the rank of Jedi Master. Twelve senior Jedi Masters form the Jedi Council, which makes decisions for the entire Jedi Order. The many species who make up the Jedi Order have expanded the varied collection of LEGO minifigures with weird and wonderful new head pieces.

Clone-trooper gloves

OBI-WAN KENOBI
Once Qui-Gon's Padawan, Obi-Wan earns honors for his skill as a negotiator during the Clone Wars.

Hair element unique to Qui-Gon

QUI-GON JINN
Qui-Gon's 2011 minifigure has lots of detail, including an updated tunic and utility belt.

Outfit has just one sleeve

AAYLA SECURA
A Twi'lek Jedi Knight, Aayla appears in Clone Turbo Tank (set 8098) in 2010. Her head top is unique.

Unique horned head top

SAESEE TIIN
Saesee's second minifigure, from Palpatine's Arrest (set 9526) in 2012, has teeth bared for combat.

Oversized binary brain

KI-ADI-MUNDI
The Cerean Jedi Ki-Adi-Mundi's minifigure has a cone head top with creases and a ponytail.

Mirialan initiate's tattoos

Barriss is adept at tandem fighting

Cape of rich fabric

▲ Barriss Offee

Barriss is a by-the-book Padawan. Her 2010 minifigure fights alongside Luminara on Geonosis and befriends Ahsoka Tano, escaping a number of wartime perils.

▼ Luminara Unduli

Mirialan Jedi Luminara Unduli's 2005 minifigure came with a light-up saber. Her 2011 minifigure, which rides a BARC speeder in the Battle of Geonosis (set 7869), has two faces and new detail on the head, torso, and legs.

Flight goggles

BARC SPEEDER

Set name	Battle for Geonosis	
Year 2011		Number 7869
Pieces 331		Source CW

Montrals (hollow head growths)

Growing head-tails

▲ Ahsoka Tano

Young Ahsoka Tano is Anakin Skywalker's Jedi Padawan during the Clone Wars. She is a Togruta—a species with colorful skin and two long "head-tails." The brown-and-gray legs on this 2010 version of Ahsoka are identical to those on Boba Fett.

Head top made of rubber

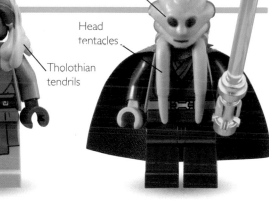

Large unblinking eyes

Tholothian tendrils

Head tentacles

AGEN KOLAR

An Iridonian Zabrak, Agen Kolar's 2012 minifigure shares a head-top design with fellow Zabrak Eeth Koth.

STASS ALLIE

This Tholothian Jedi appears in Homing Spider Droid (set 75016), in 2013. Her headdress is unique.

KIT FISTO

In 2007 Nautolan Jedi Kit Fisto was the first minifigure to have a rubber headpiece. His 2012 variant gained a cape.

MYSTERY JEDI
The end of the Clone Wars sees most Jedi killed and the Jedi Temple ransacked, with many records lost. All we know about this Jedi (whose name may have been Bob) is that he once flew on a Republic gunship (set 7163).

Full-grown head-tails

Eye lost in combat

Head crest

Gray tunic

SHAAK TI

Shaak Ti's 2011 minifigure comes with a unique rubber head piece with head-tails at front and back.

EVEN PIELL

A scarred Lannik Jedi, Even appeared with the Jedi fighter of his friend Saesee Tiin in 2012.

COLEMAN TREBOR

A hulking Vurk Jedi, Coleman fights alongside Mace Windu in the 2013 AT-TE set (75019).

JEDI BOB

Jedi Fleet

The Jedi Knights' many missions on behalf of the Republic take them across the galaxy in a variety of transports, including the diplomatic cruisers called "Coruscant reds" and agile shuttles such as the T-6. With the arrival of the Clone Wars, the Jedi take to the spacelanes in starfighters specially made for them, becoming aces in dogfights against Separatist droid fighters and other enemies.

▶ T-6 Jedi Shuttle

The T-6 shuttle's cockpit is designed to remain upright during flight maneuvers, with the wings rotating around it. Thanks to LEGO designers, Anakin Skywalker, Obi-Wan Kenobi, Shaak Ti, and Saesee Tiin can use the cockpit as an escape pod—as it detaches from the shuttle in case the craft takes too much of a beating in combat.

Wings pivot in flight mode

Hatch lifts off

Flick missile port

Sensor suite

LEGO Technic turntable, also found in fire truck and crane sets

Deflector shield generator

Republic symbol

Set name	T-6 Jedi Shuttle	
Year	2011	Number 7931
Pieces	389	Source CW

Red is a common color for Republic craft

LANDING MODE

FLIGHT MODE

▼ Republic Cruiser

The red Republic cruiser *Radiant VII* carries Qui-Gon Jinn and Obi-Wan Kenobi to their diplomatic mission on Naboo. The ship also accommodates the Republic captain and pilot minifigures, with seats for the Jedi in the detachable salon pod. The ship has hidden blaster cannons, detachable landing gear, storage for guns and electrobinoculars, and a space speeder mini-vehicle. An R2-R7 droid provides inflight backup.

Set name	Republic Cruiser	
Year	2007	Number 7665
Pieces	919	Source EP 1

Attachment point

SALON POD
An oversized escape pod below the Republic Cruiser's bridge allows Qui-Gon and Obi-Wan to flee and activate a beacon to summon help.

Pod sensors

Transmissions mast

Rotating sensor dish

Republic pilot

Sublight engine

Docking ring

Space speeder under flap

Laser cannon hatch (closed)

Hinged cockpit

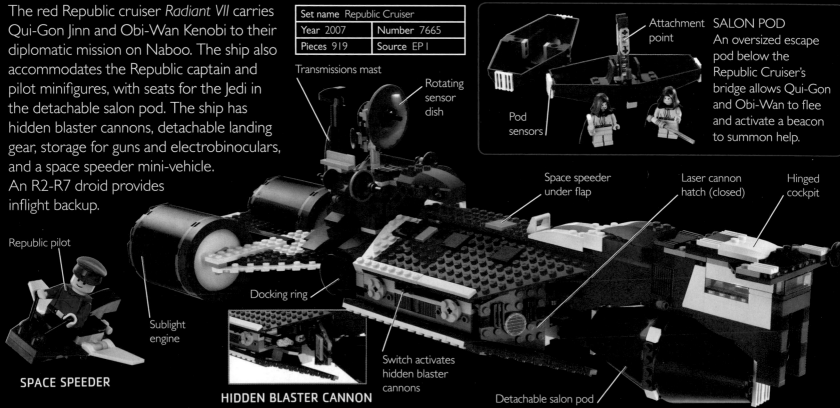

SPACE SPEEDER

Switch activates hidden blaster cannons

HIDDEN BLASTER CANNON

Detachable salon pod

Jedi Starfighters

Under the leadership of ace pilot Saesee Tiin, the Jedi train on Delta-7B *Aethersprite*-class interceptors. These are innovative strike fighters built to respond to the lightning-fast reflexes of Force-wielding Jedi. Each fighter is tailored for its pilot and has its own quirks in both the galaxy far, far away and the LEGO world: Saesee Tiin's cockpit breaks away as an escape pod, Anakin's fighter can launch R2-D2, Plo Koon's cockpit has an ejection seat, and Ahsoka Tano and Mace Windu's ships can fire multiple missiles.

Radar eye

R7-D4　　　　**R3-D5**

Hologram projector

R8-B7　　　　**R4-P44**

Linkage/repair arms

R4-P17　　　　**R7-A7**

ASTROMECHS
Astromech droids help the Jedi plot safe courses through hyperspace, repair damage to their fighters, and handle the routines of spaceflight. Some develop personalities and a rapport with their Jedi partners. Most astromechs are variants of the same standard mold, but their varied color schemes and printed details make them individuals.

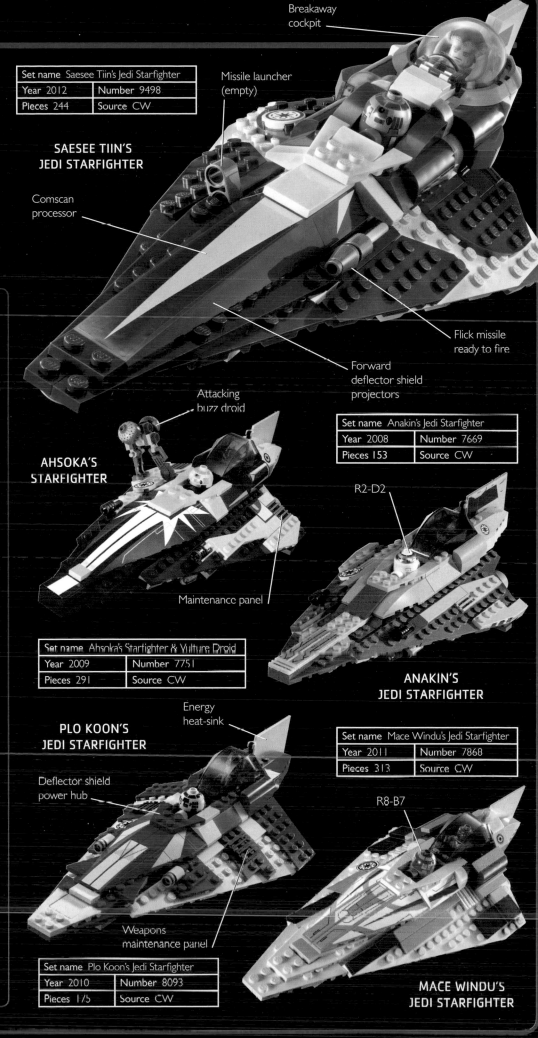

Breakaway cockpit

Missile launcher (empty)

Set name	Saesee Tiin's Jedi Starfighter	
Year 2012	Number 9498	
Pieces 244	Source CW	

SAESEE TIIN'S JEDI STARFIGHTER

Comscan processor

Flick missile ready to fire

Forward deflector shield projectors

Attacking buzz droid

AHSOKA'S STARFIGHTER

Maintenance panel

Set name	Ahsoka's Starfighter & Vulture Droid	
Year 2009	Number 7751	
Pieces 291	Source CW	

R2-D2

Set name	Anakin's Jedi Starfighter	
Year 2008	Number 7669	
Pieces 153	Source CW	

ANAKIN'S JEDI STARFIGHTER

Energy heat-sink

PLO KOON'S JEDI STARFIGHTER

Deflector shield power hub

Set name	Mace Windu's Jedi Starfighter	
Year 2011	Number 7868	
Pieces 313	Source CW	

R8-B7

Weapons maintenance panel

Set name	Plo Koon's Jedi Starfighter	
Year 2010	Number 8093	
Pieces 175	Source CW	

MACE WINDU'S JEDI STARFIGHTER

Chancellor Palpatine

Once a Senator from remote Naboo, Palpatine has cunningly risen to become Chancellor of the Republic. He has agreed to stay in office while the Republic battles the Separatists in the Clone Wars. What no one knows is that he secretly leads both sides in the conflict, and he is the hidden mastermind of the war. His true identity is Darth Sidious, the Sith Lord who seeks to destroy the Jedi and control the galaxy.

Rotate head to see Sith eyes

Robes of office

▼ *Venator*-Class Republic Attack Cruiser

The precursor to the Imperial Star Destroyer, the *Venator*-class attack cruiser has enough firepower to blast through Separatist battleships with ease. The interior hangar carries Supreme Chancellor Palpatine and two Senate commandos, while the crew comprises a clone pilot and a clone gunner.

Set name	*Venator*-Class Republic Attack Cruiser	
Year 2009	Number 8039	
Pieces 1,170	Source CW	

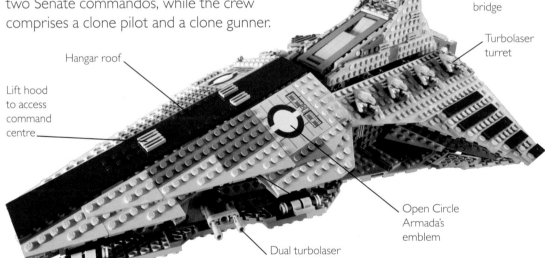

Hangar roof

Lift hood to access command centre

Command bridge

Turbolaser turret

Open Circle Armada's emblem

Dual turbolaser

▲ Palpatine's Arrest

There are two minifigures of Palpatine in his red Chancellor robes. This 2012 version has him brandishing a secret Sith lightsaber that he uses when the Jedi arrive in his office in Palpatine's Arrest (set 9526).

Set name	Separatist Shuttle	
Year 2009	Number 8036	
Pieces 259	Source CW	

Wings project deflector shield

Cockpit hood

▼ Emperor Palpatine's Shuttle

Now Emperor, Palpatine races across the galaxy in his speedy *Theta*-class shuttle to rescue a badly injured Anakin, following Anakin's duel with Obi-Wan Kenobi on Mustafar. A clone pilot accompanies the Emperor, while a 2-1B medical droid stands ready to transform Anakin into Darth Vader.

CAPTIVE LEADER
General Grievous seems to raid Coruscant and capture the Chancellor, carrying him off to his Separatist flagship.

Handcuffs

PALPATINE (KIDNAPPED)

Shield generator

Set name	Emperor Palpatine's Shuttle	
Year 2010	Number 8096	
Pieces 592	Source EP III	

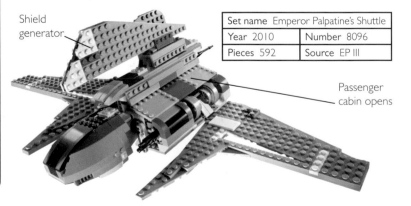

Passenger cabin opens

▲ Separatist Shuttle

Palpatine secretly commands the wealthy Trade Federation. Neimoidian puppet leader Nute Gunray travels in a *Sheathipede*-class shuttle flown by a battle droid pilot, with two battle droids for security (Neimoidians are cowardly).

Count Dooku

The lethal Sith Lord Count Dooku was once a Jedi, but lost his faith in the Jedi Order and abandoned it, eventually becoming the political leader of the Separatists. In secret, Dooku is the apprentice of Darth Sidious, and is called Darth Tyrannus. He works to advance Sidious's plot to defeat the Jedi, not suspecting that his master plans to replace him with a younger, more powerful apprentice.

SITH LORD
A noble by birth, Dooku wears an elegant cape with a silver clasp. This version of the Count, from the 2013 set Duel on Geonosis (75017), has a natural skin tone and a saber with a curved hilt.

▼ Duel on Geonosis

Dooku flees the fight on Geonosis, seeking to escape with the secret plans for the Death Star. He duels with Yoda in an abandoned factory that serves as a hangar for the Count's Solar Sailer. Aided by a long rod, Yoda's minifigure proves a nimble, acrobatic opponent—just watch out for falling columns!

Precarious column

Geonosian architecture

FA-4 pilot droid

Landing pad

Force lightning pieces

Lever controls column

Set name	Duel on Geonosis	
Year	2013	Number 75017
Pieces	391	Source EP II

▼ Dooku's Speeder Bike

Dooku's open-cockpit Flitknot speeder bike enables the Sith Lord to escape the Republic's forces on Geonosis. He flees Yoda in 2002 on a blue version and later uses two brown, more streamlined, versions.

Control panel

Seat

Throttle

SET HISTORY

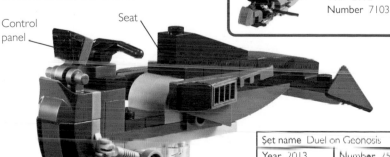

Count Dooku's Solar Sailer
Year 2009
Number 7752

Jedi Duel
Year 2002
Number 7103

Set name	Duel on Geonosis	
Year	2013	Number 75017
Pieces	391	Source EP II

▼ Solar Sailer

Count Dooku's personal starship is an elegant Geonosian Solar Sailer, piloted by a FA-4 droid. Dooku and two MagnaGuards travel to battlefields, where Dooku then uses his speeder bike to meet Separatist leaders.

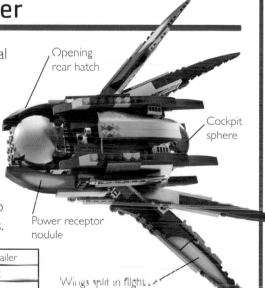

Opening rear hatch

Cockpit sphere

Power receptor nodule

Wings split in flight

Set name	Count Dooku's Solar Sailer	
Year	2009	Number 7752
Pieces	385	Source CW

Sith Followers

REAR VIEW

Open hatch

Cockpit

"Always two there are. A Master and an apprentice." Yoda explains that for millennia, the secret Sith Order has preserved itself by passing down teachings and waiting for the right time to overthrow the Jedi and seize galactic control. But the Sith are deceitful by nature, with apprentices always plotting against their masters. And Masters recruit beyond their apprentice to find other followers to do their bidding.

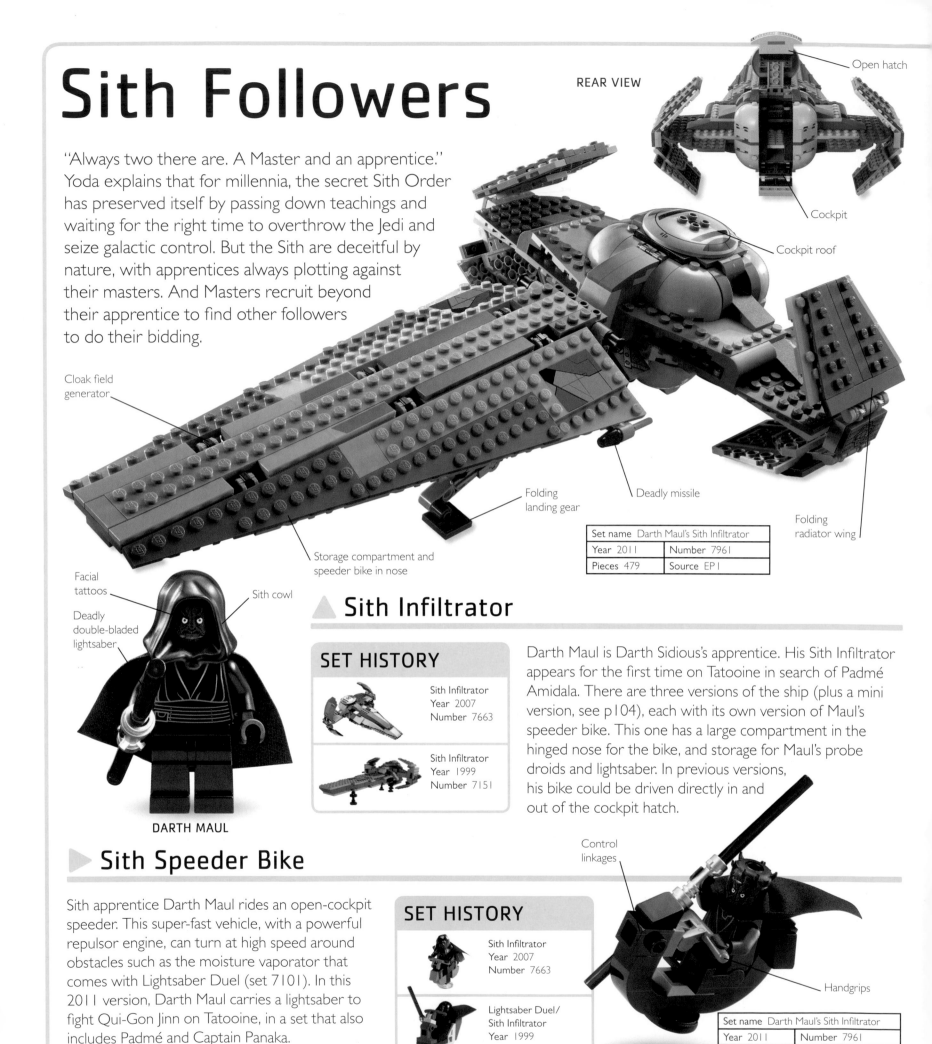

Cockpit roof

Cloak field generator

Folding landing gear

Deadly missile

Folding radiator wing

Storage compartment and speeder bike in nose

Set name	Darth Maul's Sith Infiltrator	
Year 2011	Number	7961
Pieces 479	Source	EP1

Facial tattoos

Sith cowl

Deadly double-bladed lightsaber

▲ Sith Infiltrator

DARTH MAUL

SET HISTORY

Sith Infiltrator
Year 2007
Number 7663

Sith Infiltrator
Year 1999
Number 7151

Darth Maul is Darth Sidious's apprentice. His Sith Infiltrator appears for the first time on Tatooine in search of Padmé Amidala. There are three versions of the ship (plus a mini version, see p104), each with its own version of Maul's speeder bike. This one has a large compartment in the hinged nose for the bike, and storage for Maul's probe droids and lightsaber. In previous versions, his bike could be driven directly in and out of the cockpit hatch.

Control linkages

▶ Sith Speeder Bike

Sith apprentice Darth Maul rides an open-cockpit speeder. This super-fast vehicle, with a powerful repulsor engine, can turn at high speed around obstacles such as the moisture vaporator that comes with Lightsaber Duel (set 7101). In this 2011 version, Darth Maul carries a lightsaber to fight Qui-Gon Jinn on Tatooine, in a set that also includes Padmé and Captain Panaka.

SET HISTORY

Sith Infiltrator
Year 2007
Number 7663

Lightsaber Duel/
Sith Infiltrator
Year 1999
Number 7101/7151

Handgrips

Set name	Darth Maul's Sith Infiltrator	
Year 2011	Number	7961
Pieces 479	Source	EP1

Sith Nightspeeder

The Dathomirian Asajj Ventress rides a fearsome speeder bike with a spiked hull while on a mission for the Nightsisters, witches who rule her home world of Dathomir. In battle, Asajj's bike and its sidecar can split off from the hulking portside engine pod, which can launch missiles at enemies. Asajj returns aboard the nightspeeder with Savage Opress—a warrior who will serve Count Dooku, but remain secretly loyal to the Nightsisters, who seek revenge on Dooku for his betrayal of Asajj.

Set name	Sith Nightspeeder	
Year	2011	Number 7957
Pieces	213	Source CW

Waste-heat vents

Sidecar

Control linkages

Turbojet pod

Nightsister design

Missile port

DARTH MAUL (APPRENTICE)

SITH APPRENTICE
Darth Sidious trained Maul from infanthood, using cruelty and trickery to turn the young Zabrak into a ruthless, terrifying warrior who would be an instrument of his will. As Sidious's sinister agent, Maul struck without warning against his Master's enemies. This minifigure, with Zabrak horns and a tattooed face and torso, was released in a promotional polybag (set 5000062) in 2012.

Darth Maul

Maul somehow survived being cut in half by Obi-Wan Kenobi, fleeing into the Outer Rim but losing his sanity in exile. After Savage Opress found him, the Nightsisters' magic healed his mind and created cybernetic legs for him. Joined by Savage, Maul tried to take over the galactic underworld. This intimidating 2013 figure with unique leg pieces is from the Mandalorian Speeder (set 75022).

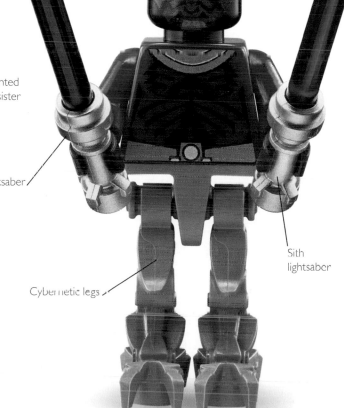

Detachable headpiece

Darksaber

Cybernetic legs

Sith lightsaber

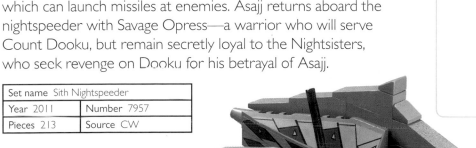

Facial tattoos

One of two sabers

Double-bladed saber

Zabrak horns

Enchanted Nightsister blade

Asajj Ventress

Asajj once trained as a Jedi, but turned to the dark side after the death of her Master, becoming Dooku's servant. She fights using twin lightsabers. Asajj and Savage Opress come with the Sith Nightspeeder (set 7957), released in 2011.

Savage Opress

A Nightbrother from Dathomir, Savage was transformed into a deadly warrior by dark-side magic. Infuriated by Dooku's training and the Nightsisters' scheming, he fled in search of his lost brother, Darth Maul, who became his new teacher.

Republic Army

For generations, the Republic had no army, relying only on the Jedi Knights to maintain peace and justice in the galaxy. But the vast Separatist Droid Army forced Republic leaders to take decisive action. The Republic quickly amassed one of the largest armies ever seen, with millions of clone troopers led by Jedi generals and diverse, specialized vehicles designed for missions on the ground.

Set name	AT-RT	
Year 2013		Number 75002
Pieces 222		Source CW

Repeating blaster

▲ AT-RT Walker

The All Terrain Recon Transport (AT-RT), or scout walker, is an open-cockpit recon vehicle.

SET HISTORY

Clone Turbo Tank
Year 2010
Number 8098

Clone Walker
Battle Pack
Year 2009
Number 8014

Clone Scout
Walker
Year 2005
Number 7250

▼ AT-AP Walker

The All Terrain Attack Pod (AT-AP) is a two-legged walker, though both LEGO versions have a third, retractable, stabilizer leg. It is equipped with massive blaster cannons; the roof and side doors open to reveal an interior cabin.

Elevating cannon

Repeating blaster

SET HISTORY

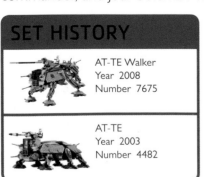

AT-AP Walker
Year 2008
Number 7671

Set name	AT-AP Walker	
Year 2014		Number 75043
Pieces 717		Source EP III

▲ AV-7 Anti-Vehicle Cannon

These artillery units reposition themselves by shuffling on their four heavy legs, then spreading their feet to take the shock of blasts from the cannon barrel. They are effective against both enemy ground units and aircraft.

Power leads

Cannon axis housing

Feet allow repositioning

Set name	Republic AV-7 Anti-Vehicle Cannon	
Year 2014		Number 75045
Pieces 434		Source CW

▼ AT-TE Walker

The six-legged All Terrain Tactical Enforcer, or AT-TE Walker, blasts ground or air targets with massive cannons, while six laser cannon turrets focus on smaller targets. This set features four minifigures: two battle droids, a clone commander, and Jedi Coleman Trebor.

Set name	AT-TE	
Year 2013		Number 75019
Pieces 794		Source EP II

Gunner's station

Heavy projectile cannon

Bar step access to cabin

Cabin slides out

Laser cannon turret

Hinged roof lifts up

Servomotor disc

Terrain sensors

SET HISTORY

AT-TE Walker
Year 2008
Number 7675

AT-TE
Year 2003
Number 4482

▼ Fighter Tank

The TX-130 *Saber*-class fighter vehicle is a fast-attack tank equipped with laser cannons and concussion missiles. Clone troopers pilot this tank, though many Jedi also drive them during the Clone Wars.

Flick-fire laser cannon

Sensor antenna

"Hovers" on hidden wheels

Clone soldier on patrol

Set name	Republic Fighter Tank	
Year 2008	Number 7679	
Pieces 592	Source CW	

SET HISTORY

Clone Trooper Battle Pack/Battle for Geonosis
Year 2011
Number 7913/7869

Clone Troopers Battle Pack
Year 2007
Number 7655

Clone Turbo Tank
Year 2005
Number 7261

▼ BARC Speeder

This two-person Biker Advanced Recon Commando (BARC) speeder often escorts gunships carrying important passengers. Propelled by repulsors and a turbine engine, the bike is armed with two pairs of blasters on each side and a pair of ion cannons.

Set name	Kashyyyk Troopers	
Year 2014	Number 75035	
Pieces 99	Source CW	

Control yokes

Stabilizer fins

▼ Swamp Speeder

Formally known as an Infantry Support Platform, or ISP, the Swamp Speeder uses its giant turbofan and repulsorlifts to race through marshy terrain.

SET HISTORY

Kashyyyk Troopers
Year 2014
Number 75035

Wookiee Catamaran
Year 2005
Number 7260

Set name	Republic Swamp Speeder	
Year 2010	Number 8091	
Pieces 176	Source EP III	

Mudshield

PILOT TO GUNNER

A 2013 variant model of the BARC Speeder includes a sidecar, allowing a gunner to shoot down enemies while the pilot flies (set 75012).

Obi-Wan's lightsaber

SPEEDER WITH SIDECAR

▼ Turbo Tank

SET HISTORY

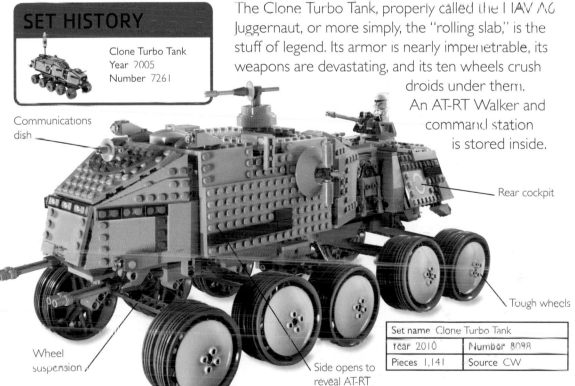

Clone Turbo Tank
Year 2005
Number 7261

The Clone Turbo Tank, properly called the HAV A6 Juggernaut, or more simply, the "rolling slab," is the stuff of legend. Its armor is nearly impenetrable, its weapons are devastating, and its ten wheels crush droids under them.
An AT-RT Walker and command station is stored inside.

Communications dish

Rear cockpit

Wheel suspension

Side opens to reveal AT-RT

Tough wheels

Set name	Clone Turbo Tank	
Year 2010	Number 8098	
Pieces 1,141	Source CW	

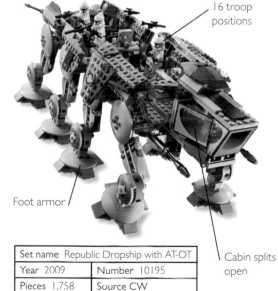

16 troop positions

Foot armor

Cabin splits open

▲ AT-OT Walker

Set name	Republic Dropship with AT-OT	
Year 2009	Number 10195	
Pieces 1,758	Source CW	

Open-topped All Terrain Open Transports (AT-OTs) are not designed to be tanks, but to transport troops and cargo in safe zones.

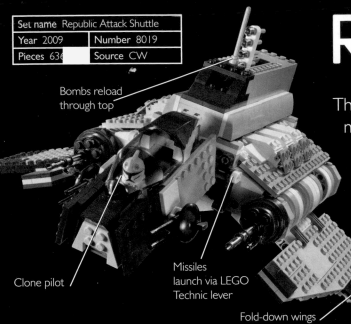

Set name	Republic Attack Shuttle	
Year	2009	Number 8019
Pieces	636	Source CW

Bombs reload through top

Clone pilot

Missiles launch via LEGO Technic lever

Fold-down wings

Republic Navy

The Republic defends its spacelanes and millions of worlds with a massive navy composed of giant warships, smaller transports and gunships, and sleek, speedy starfighters. Navy personnel include both clone officers and non-clones drawn from many species. These brave beings clash with Count Dooku's Separatist starships above countless planets as the Clone Wars rage.

▼ Z-95 Headhunter

Clones serving Jedi General Pong Krell pilot Z-95s in the Battle of Umbara. The LEGO version flies into battle with retractable landing gear, a weapons locker, and a LEGO Technic missile.

Weapons locker

Sensor suite

Set name	Z-95 Headhunter	
Year	2013	Number 75004
Pieces	373	Source CW

▲ Republic Attack Shuttle

The *Nu*-class attack shuttle is a fast, long-range gunship, with heavy armor, powerful shields, and a range of laser weaponry, though this model is also equipped to drop missiles from a bomb hatch on the underside. A clone pilot flies the ship, which carries Mace Windu and a clone trooper into battle.

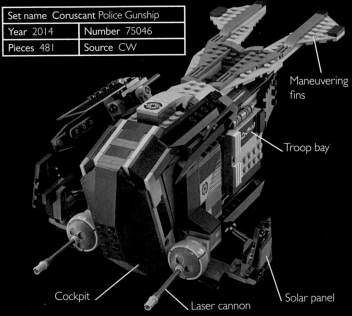

Set name	Coruscant Police Gunship	
Year	2014	Number 75046
Pieces	481	Source CW

Maneuvering fins

Troop bay

Cockpit

Laser cannon

Solar panel

▼ Republic Frigate

Most Republic frigates were originally consular ships used by ambassadors and diplomats for galaxy-wide missions. With the galaxy torn apart by war, the Republic upgraded these vessels for battle. This ship comes with flick-fire missles, a mechanism for dropping three further missiles in bombing raids, gun turrets, and a detachable escape pod.

Missile launcher

Hatch under paneling

Navigational sensor dish

Forward sensors

Detachable escape pod

Set name	Republic Frigate	
Year	2011	Number 7964
Pieces	1,015	Source CW

▲ Police Gunship

Fast and maneuverable, police gunships respond to trouble on the Republic capital of Coruscant. They are less heavily armed than attack gunships, as avoiding damage to crowded city blocks is more important than the ability to unleash a heavy bombardment. Clone troopers sometimes command these craft for military missions.

ARC-170 Starfighter

The Aggressive ReConnaissance (ARC-170) fighter is hyperdrive-equipped for long-range missions. The 2010 ship's crew consists of Kit Fisto, Captain Jag, a clone pilot, and an R4 astromech. The ship's wings unfold when in flight, while mines can be dropped from the underside.

Hinged cockpit screen

Wing-mounted laser cannon

Red styling

Heat sinks and cooling radiator panels on split wings

Set name	ARC-170 Starfighter	
Year	2010	Number 8088
Pieces	356	Source CW

CAPTAIN JAG

Clone pilots such as Jag are chosen early in the training cycle after demonstrating superior eyesight, reflexes, and spatial awareness. Jag serves Jedi Plo Koon as a wingman.

Dropship

Turbine

LEGO Technic carry pin for AT-OT

Nose art (choice of stickers)

Communications antenna

Low Altitude Assault Transport/carriers (LAAT/c or dropships) carry tanks into battlezones. This 2009 ship can lift and carry the AT-OT (see p31) from this set with the use of LEGO Technic mechanisms.

Set name	Republic Dropship with AT-OT	
Year	2009	Number 10195
Pieces	1,758	Source CW

Laser cannon

Concussion missile launcher

Powerful thruster

Set name	V-19 Torrent	
Year	2008	Number 7674
Pieces	471	Source CW

Ventral airfoil

Radiator panel wing

Sublight engine

Ignition chamber

V-19 Torrent Starfighter

This fast, agile assault fighter features wing-mounted laser cannons and concussion missile launchers. The wings extend in flight and close for landing, allowing the clone pilot access to the cockpit via a sliding hatch.

Portside guns

Bomb chamber

V-Wing Starfighter

Clone troopers pilot agile V-wing fighters, with spherical Q7 astromechs as copilots. The wings unfold in flight and the laser cannons are powerful and deadly.

EETH KOTH

Swiveling laser cannons

Set name	V-Wing Starfighter	
Year	2014	Number 75039
Pieces	201	Source CW

Wings in flying mode

Forward sensors

Clone Troopers

At the start of the Clone Wars, clone troopers wear Phase I armor, which is loosely based on Jango Fett's Mandalorian shock trooper armor. Informally called "the body bucket," this armor is heavy and often uncomfortable. Colored stripes denote rank. During the later part of the Clone Wars, Phase II armor mainly replaces Phase I armor. Phase II armor is stronger, lighter, and more adaptable than the earlier type, with many specialist variations. Color now denotes unit affiliation rather than rank.

ANATOMY OF A CLONE TROOPER
"Explode" this ARC trooper from Elite Clone Trooper and Commando Droid Battle Pack (set 9488) and you see just how complex a simple minifigure can get!

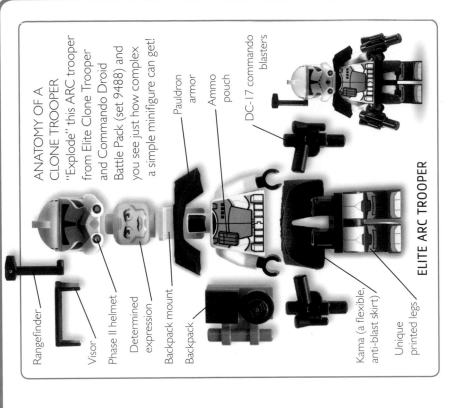

- Rangefinder
- Visor
- Phase II helmet
- Determined expression
- Backpack mount
- Backpack
- Pauldron armor
- Ammo pouch
- DC-17 commando blasters
- Kama (a flexible, anti-blast skirt)
- Unique printed legs

ELITE ARC TROOPER

▶ Phase I Clone Troopers

Phase I clone trooper minifigures wear basic white armor with white helmets. Early Phase I clones had a faceless black head piece and carried a loudhailer for a weapon. In 2008, a new version of the Phase I clone minifigure gave them flesh-colored heads and bespoke blasters. A variant Phase I clone has a jetpack for aerial operations.

- "T" visor derived from Mandalorian design

CLONE TROOPER (PHASE I)

- DC-15 rifle

CLONE CAPTAIN

- Life-support pack

CLONE PILOT

- Specially reinforced helmet

BOMB SQUAD TROOPER

- Dots indicate rank

CLONE SERGEANT

CLONE LIEUTENANT

▶ Phase I Clone Commanders

Promising clones are discovered early on in their production and are given special training, with more individuality than the troops they command. Commanders such as Fox, Cody, and Wolffe work closely with Jedi generals in the fight against the Separatists.

- Visor shield unique to LEGO commanders

COMMANDER CODY

- Rangefinder

COMMANDER FOX

COMMANDER WOLFFE

COMMANDER (HORN COMPANY)

▶ Phase II Clone Troopers

Later in the Clone Wars, the Republic created improved Phase II armor with improved breath filter/annunciators. Minifigures' heads are plain black under the helmets. Camouflage is sometimes used on Phase II armor.

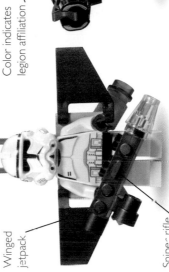

Air supply nozzles

Utility belt

Printed legs

CLONE TROOPER (PHASE II)

Color indicates legion affiliation

212TH TROOPER

Winged jetpack

Sniper rifle

AERIAL TROOPER

CLONE PILOT

Specialized helmet

SHOCKTROOPER

CLONE PARATROOPER

Heat dispersion vent

501ST TROOPER

STAR CORPS TROOPER

NEW WEAPONS

For 2014, there was a new LEGO clone sidearm, with a translucent blue round plate at the muzzle—a feature also found on the first clone weapons.

Trigger mechanism launches stud

Translucent stud

ELITE CLONE TROOPERS

As clone troopers pursue specialized missions, the Republic develops new helmets and armor for these units. Advanced Recon Force troopers are trained for stealth, with infrared cameras built into their helmets. A variant ARF trooper LEGO minifigure has white shoulder and forearm armor and green helmet markings.

Night-vision lenses

Specialized breathing gear

Unit markings

Enhanced comlink

Rifle for long-range combat

ELITE ARF TROOPER

▶ Phase II Clone Commanders

By the end of the Clone Wars, many clone commanders are veterans of years of battle and have formed close relationships with their Jedi generals. When Chancellor Palpatine issues Order 66 these friendships mean nothing. Obeying their insidious conditioning and training, clone commanders turn their guns on the Jedi they have served on so many missions.

Pauldron

Anti-blast kama

"Jaig eyes" are a battlefield honor

Rex wields twin blasters

CAPTAIN REX

Enhanced breath filter

COMMANDER NEYO

Separatist Army

Although mass armies are illegal at the start of the Clone Wars, many wealthy commercial bodies use private forces to enforce payments and collect debts. These forces are pooled to create the Separatist war machine, under the command of Count Dooku. Consisting of huge numbers of deadly droids backed by attack vehicles, the Separatist army assaults Republic worlds from one side of the galaxy to the other.

Droid Speeder

The commando droid on this speeder chases Obi-Wan and Captain Rex in 2013. The earlier 2011 version of the bike is used by a TX-20 tactical droid to ambush Mace Windu's Jedi starfighter.

SET HISTORY

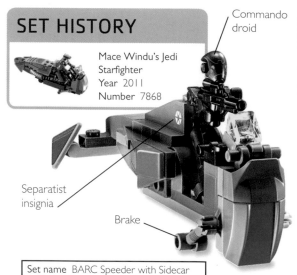

Mace Windu's Jedi Starfighter
Year 2011
Number 7868

Commando droid

Separatist insignia

Brake

Set name BARC Speeder with Sidecar	
Year 2013	Number 75012
Pieces 226	Source CW

MECHANICAL MARVEL
Programmed to think up ideal strategies for the battlefield, tactical droids assist the flesh-and-blood generals of the Separatist cause.

TACTICAL DROID

SET HISTORY

Trade Federation ATT
Year 2000
Number 7155

Armored Assault Tank

The 2009 repulsorlift AAT glides into battle armed with laser weapons and carrying two battle droids and three dark-gray super battle droids (who face off against Yoda and a clone trooper). A speeder bike can be deployed from the rear for high-speed strike/reconnaissance missions.

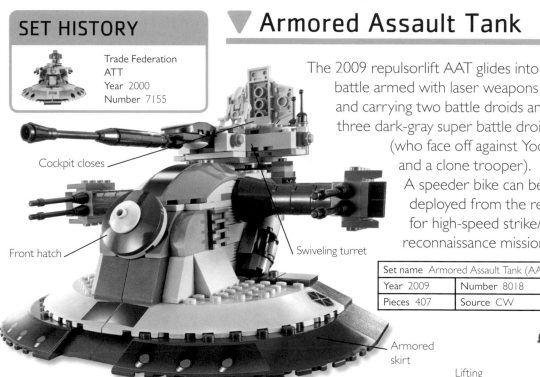

Cockpit closes

Front hatch

Swiveling turret

Armored skirt

Set name Armored Assault Tank (AAT)	
Year 2009	Number 8018
Pieces 407	Source CW

MTT

The larger, updated MTT carries 20 battle droids. Turning the side gear deploys the droid storage rack, while various exterior panels are hinged to allow access to the interior. A separate troop carrier deploys from a hatch in the back for the rapid transport of battle-ready droids. The set includes 16 regular battle droids, two red security droids, two blue pilot droids, and a droideka.

SET HISTORY

Trade Federation MTT
Year 2000
Number 7184

Lifting cockpit hatch

Pilot droid in cockpit

Side hatch

Troop carrier deploys from hatch in rear

Hinged troop deployment hatch

Sliding rack

Folded battle droids

Side gear (deploys droid storage rack)

Troop carrier

Engine housing

Set name Trade Federation MTT	
Year 2007	Number 7662
Pieces 1,330	Source EP1

Infantry Battle Droid

Infantry battle droids make up the majority of the Separatist land troops. Early versions of the minifigure have two identical hands. From 2007 onward, battle droid minifigures have had a turned hand in order to properly hold a blaster.

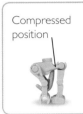 

Compressed position

COLLAPSIBLE SOLDIERS
Battle droid minifigures fold up for efficient storage in deployment racks in MTTs and other carriers.

STAP

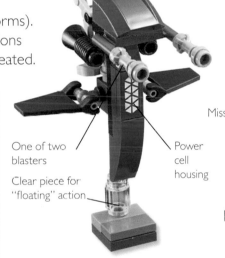

Battle droids pilot repulsorlift gun platforms called STAPs (Single Trooper Aerial Platforms). Brown and blue LEGO versions of the vehicles have been created.

One of two blasters

Power cell housing

Clear piece for "floating" action

Set name	Battle on Saleucami	
Year 2014	Number 75037	
Pieces 178	Source CW	

SET HISTORY

Droids Battle Pack
Year 2007
Number 7654

Battle Droid Carrier
Year 2001
Number 7126

Drive unit

Headlight swivels

Weapon rack

Battle droid in compressed form

Rack unclamps and slides free

Set name	The Battle of Naboo	
Year 2011	Number 7929	
Pieces 241	Source EP I	

Droid Transports

Separatist troop carriers ferry battle droids to the battlefield more quickly than bulky MTT transports. Two battle-droid pilots control the troop carrier, deploying eight battle droids folded up to save space. This model of troop carrier is unarmed, relying on its speed to escape Gungan warriors and other enemies.

Octuptarra Droid

Missile

Multiple photoreceptors and blasters give these stilt-legged droids the ability to detect and target enemies on all sides of them, making them tough opponents. Octuptarras defended General Grievous's headquarters against the Republic's clone troopers on Utapau.

Hydraulic limb

Set name	Utapau Troopers	
Year 2014	Number 75036	
Pieces 83	Source CW	

SUPER BATTLE DROIDS
Super battle droids are larger, stronger versions of regular battle droids. They are also equipped with tougher armor. There are three versions of the minifigure in different colors; one with specially molded blaster arms.

METAL-BLUE (2002)	DARK-GRAY (2007)	BLASTER-ARM (2009)

Separatist Cannon

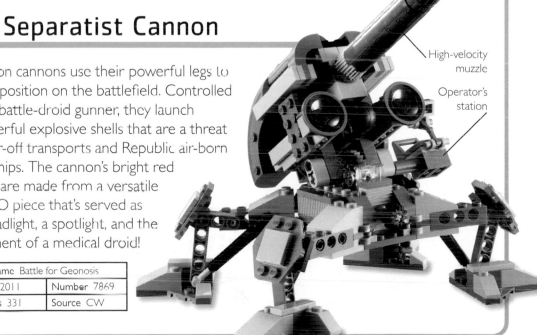

Proton cannons use their powerful legs to shift position on the battlefield. Controlled by a battle-droid gunner, they launch powerful explosive shells that are a threat to far-off transports and Republic air-born gunships. The cannon's bright red eyes are made from a versatile LEGO piece that's served as a headlight, a spotlight, and the segment of a medical droid!

High-velocity muzzle

Operator's station

Set name	Battle for Geonosis	
Year 2011	Number 7869	
Pieces 331	Source CW	

▼ Droideka

Destroyer droids, or droidekas, roll into battle, uncurl, and then deploy built-in blasters to deadly effect. So far, droideka models have battled clones in seven LEGO sets, with the droids looking more and more like their on-screen counterparts. An intriguing variant is the long-barreled Sniper Droideka, able to target distant enemies. It's found in the AT-RT (set 75002) released in 2013.

Battlefield Droids

For years, the galaxy's wealthy, unsavory corporations enforced their will on customers with terrifying weaponized droids designed to collect debts, force labor settlements, and eliminate rivals. When those corporations join together to form the Separatist alliance, their droids become the muscle of the armies sent to invade Republic worlds, with Separatist factories working overtime to turn out new models.

SET HISTORY

	AT-RT Year 2013 Number 75002
	Clone Troopers vs. Droidekas Year 2013 Number 75000
	Naboo Starfighter Year 2011 Number 7877
	Trade Federation MTT Year 2007 Number 7662
	Republic Gunship / Jedi Defense I Year 2002 Number 7163 / 7203

Backshell plate

Switch used as eyestalk

Foot claw

Set name	Republic AV-7 Anti-Vehicle Cannon	
Year	2014	Number 75045
Pieces	434	Source CW

▼ Dwarf Spider Droid

Dwarf spider droids are mobile laser cannon turrets that walk into battle in advance of battle droids. While not very smart, these droids sometimes refuse to advance when badly outnumbered by enemies.

SET HISTORY

	Hailfire Droid & Spider Droid Year 2008 Number 7670
	Wookiee Attack Year 2005 Number 7258

Tracing antenna

Infrared photoreceptor

Laser cannon

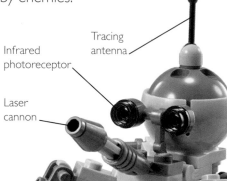

Set name	Homing Spider Droid	
Year	2013	Number 75016
Pieces	295	Source EP II

Hinged knee joint

Clawed feet

Hinged racks

Flick-fire missiles

Photoreceptor

Hoop wheels straighten up for travel

Drive unit

Clear discs hold treads together

◄ Hailfire Droid

Hailfire droids roll into battle on giant hoop wheels while firing deadly heat-seeking missiles from two top-mounted racks. The Hailfire's red photoreceptor sees in the infrared spectrum, determines range to a target, and then feeds that data to the systems controlling its weapons.

Set name	Hailfire Droid & Spider Droid	
Year	2008	Number 7670
Pieces	249	Source EP II

Tank Droid

Amphibious NR-N99 tank droids roll into battle on high-traction caterpillar treads. Three LEGO versions of the tank have been deployed: on Kashyyk in 2005, one for the new *Clone Wars* movie in 2009, and this one on Geonosis in 2013. Deployed side by side, they form an unstoppable wall of armor, obliterating everything in their path.

SET HISTORY

Corporate Alliance
Tank Droid
Year 2009
Number 7748

Wookiee Attack
Year 2005
Number 7258

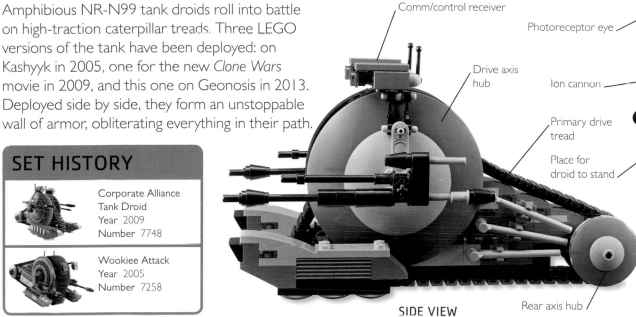

Comm/control receiver

Drive axis hub

Photoreceptor eye

Ion cannon

Primary drive tread

Place for droid to stand

FRONT VIEW

Pontoon

60 tread pieces

SIDE VIEW

Rear axis hub

Set name	Corporate Alliance Tank Droid	
Year 2013	Number 75015	
Pieces 271	Source EP II	

Moveable surface-to-air missile

◀ Spider Droid

SET HISTORY

Separatist Spider
Droid
Year 2008
Number 7681

Homing spider droids can cover great distances on their all-terrain legs. Their sensors lock on to enemy targets and their dish-shaped laser cannons provide sustained fire. The equator of the droid's head is repurposed from a wheel found in several LEGO motorcycle sets, a clever reuse that lets the top and bottom pieces rotate.

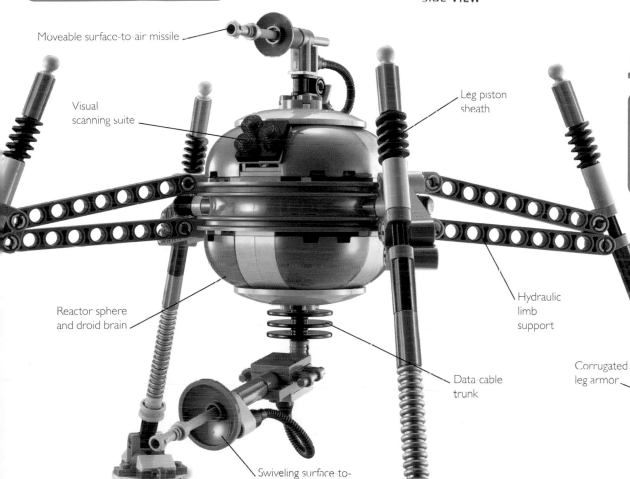

Visual scanning suite

Leg piston sheath

Reactor sphere and droid brain

Hydraulic limb support

Data-cable trunk

Corrugated leg armor

Swiveling surface-to-surface laser cannon

Swiveling ankle joint

All-terrain footpad

BRICK FACTS

Are droideka parts edible? Well, the 2013 model's central eye appears as a cherry atop a cupcake in SpongeBob™ SquarePants's Bikini Bottom Sea Party (set 3818), while its backshell is a smear of chocolate icing in the Birthday Cake (set 40048).

Set name	Homing Spider Droid	
Year 2013	Number 75016	
Pieces 295	Source EP II	

Separatist Navy

After their first success at the Battle of Geonosis, Separatist forces plot and scheme even greater exploits. The gigantic space battle above Coruscant, in which General Grievous attempts to kidnap Supreme Chancellor Palpatine, sees the use of a deadly range of specialized droid fighters. Other Separatist units batter enemy ground forces and civilian targets on contested planets such as Kashyyyk and Ryloth.

Reactor core

Maneuvering thrusters

Set name	Droid Gunship	
Year	2014	Number 75042
Pieces	439	Source EP II & CW

▶ Droid Gunship

Droid gunships are well-shielded heavy missile platforms (HMPs) designed for sub-orbital air strikes. They are relatively slow to maneuver but their firepower is devastating. Droid brains usually control the gunships, but some modified versions include a cockpit for a battle droid pilot.

Long-range sensor ports

Hinged weapons module

Medium laser cannon

Rotating laser cannon turret

SET HISTORY

Droid Gunship
Year 2008
Number 7678

▼ Vulture Droid

SET HISTORY

Ahsoka's Starfighter & Vulture Droid
Year 2009
Number 7751

Naboo N-1 Starfighter & Vulture Droid
Year 2007
Number 7660

Jedi Starfighter & Vulture Droid
Year 2005
Number 7256

Droid Fighter
Year 1999
Number 7111

The Trade Federation defends its battleships with swarms of these pilot-less droid fighters, controlled by signals from a central Droid Control Ship. Vulture droids can also reorient their heads and walk on their wingtips, doing double duty as effective, if somewhat ungainly, patrol units. Not particularly intelligent, vulture droids overwhelm enemies through sheer numbers.

Set name	Vulture Droid	
Year	2014	Number 75041
Pieces	205	Source EP III & CW

Claw wing

Head swivels in landing mode

Wings convert to legs

Active sensor "eyes"

Spring-loaded shooter under vessel

Laser cannon

FLIGHT AND WALK MODE
In flight mode, the Vulture droid's wings retract to conceal weapons. When the ship lands, the wings reconfigure into walk mode.

WALKING MODE

FLYING MODE

WALKING MODE

Droid brain unit

Target scoping suite

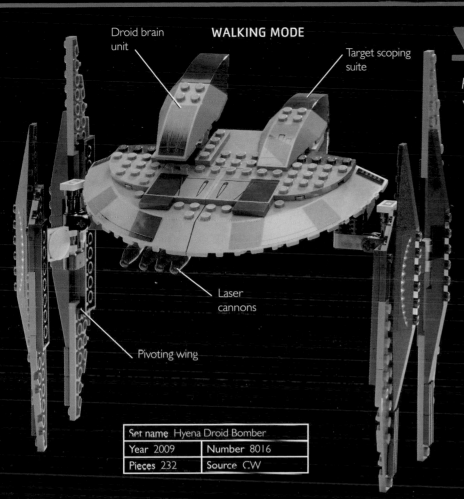

Laser cannons

Pivoting wing

Set name	Hyena Droid Bomber	
Year 2009	Number 8016	
Pieces 232	Source C.W	

Hyena Droid Bomber

Hyena-class droid bombers are modified vulture fighters, with a secondary cockpit sensor "head" for improved target scoping and upgraded weapons systems, including concussion missile launchers. Notoriously, hyena droid bombers performed carpet-bombing raids on Twi'lek cities during the Battle of Ryloth.

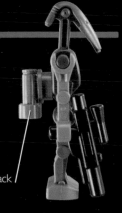

Jetpack

ROCKET BATTLE DROID

Torpedo channel

Concussion missiles drop from underneath

FLYING MODE

ROCKET BATTLE DROIDS
These modified B1 battle droids are designed for scouting missions deep in space. They hunt down and destroy enemies fleeing in escape pods. Commanders are recognizable by a yellow marking on their head.

Color indicates rank

ROCKET BATTLE DROID COMMANDER

Swiveling wing blaster

Droid Tri-Fighter

SET HISTORY

Droid Tri-Fighter
Year 2010
Number 8086

Droid Tri-Fighter
Year 2005
Number 7252

Cockpit

Nose laser cannon

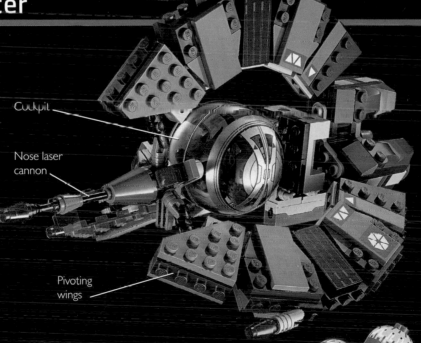

Pivoting wings

With a nose-mounted laser cannon and three light laser cannons, droid tri-fighters are deadlier than vulture droids. These agile, fast droids excel at dogfights with Republic starfighters. Some modified tri-fighters are piloted by battle droids that sit in their central spheres.

Set name	Droid Tri-Fighter	
Year 2014	Number 75044	
Pieces 262	Source EP II & III	

SPRING-LOADED MISSILE LAUNCHER

BUZZ DROID
Separatist fighters launch swarms of buzz droids as guided missiles. They hunt for enemy ships, slip through shields, and wreak havoc with their saws and graspers.

Outer shell

Saw

General Grievous

The Supreme Commander of the Droid Armies is a villainous cyborg called General Grievous. Grievous does not consider himself a droid, however—and reacts savagely to anyone who calls him one. His hatred of the Jedi Knights in particular is long-standing and all-consuming. His only pleasure is defeating Jedi in battle and collecting their lightsabers as trophies.

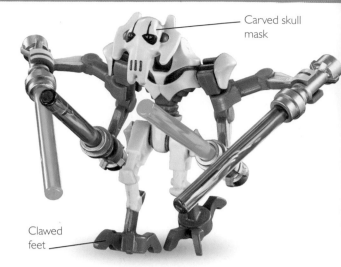

Carved skull mask

Clawed feet

GENERAL GRIEVOUS

The first two Grievous minifigures used mostly battle droid parts. In 2010, a more specialized minifigure was created in tan, which was then turned white in 2014.

Set name	The *Malevolence*	
Year 2012	Number 9515	
Pieces 1092	Source CW	

▼ Malevolence

General Grievous's flagship, the *Malevolence*, is one of the largest warships ever built. It strikes terror into Republic worlds, with no fleet able to stand up to its massive twin ion cannons, backed up with turbolasers. The *subjugator*-class heavy cruiser has an internal transport train and the top of the LEGO model lifts off to reveal the inner ship.

Bridge

Handle

Hull opens to reveal hover train

Engine thrusters

Power generator

Flick-missile launcher

Ion cannon emplacement

▶ Wheel Bike

On Utapau, General Grievous rides a wheel bike, designed to achieve intimidatingly high speeds across hard terrain. If obstacles block its path, no problem—its two pairs of legs just walk over them! When Grievous flees clone troops on Utapau, Obi-Wan Kenobi gives chase on Boga, a brave varactyl.

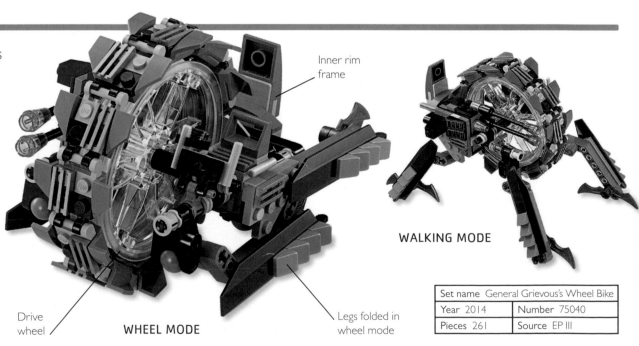

Inner rim frame

WALKING MODE

Drive wheel

WHEEL MODE

Legs folded in wheel mode

SET HISTORY

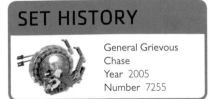

General Grievous Chase
Year 2005
Number 7255

Set name	General Grievous's Wheel Bike	
Year 2014	Number 75040	
Pieces 261	Source EP III	

Grievous's Starfighter

General Grievous's battle-worn Belbullab-22 fighter is hyperdrive-capable and features a sliding cockpit, folding tail landing gear, and flip-up laser cannons. Missile launchers hidden inside the wings flip open during combat. When not aboard his fighter, Grievous directs operations from his command chair, keeping his lightsabers close at hand.

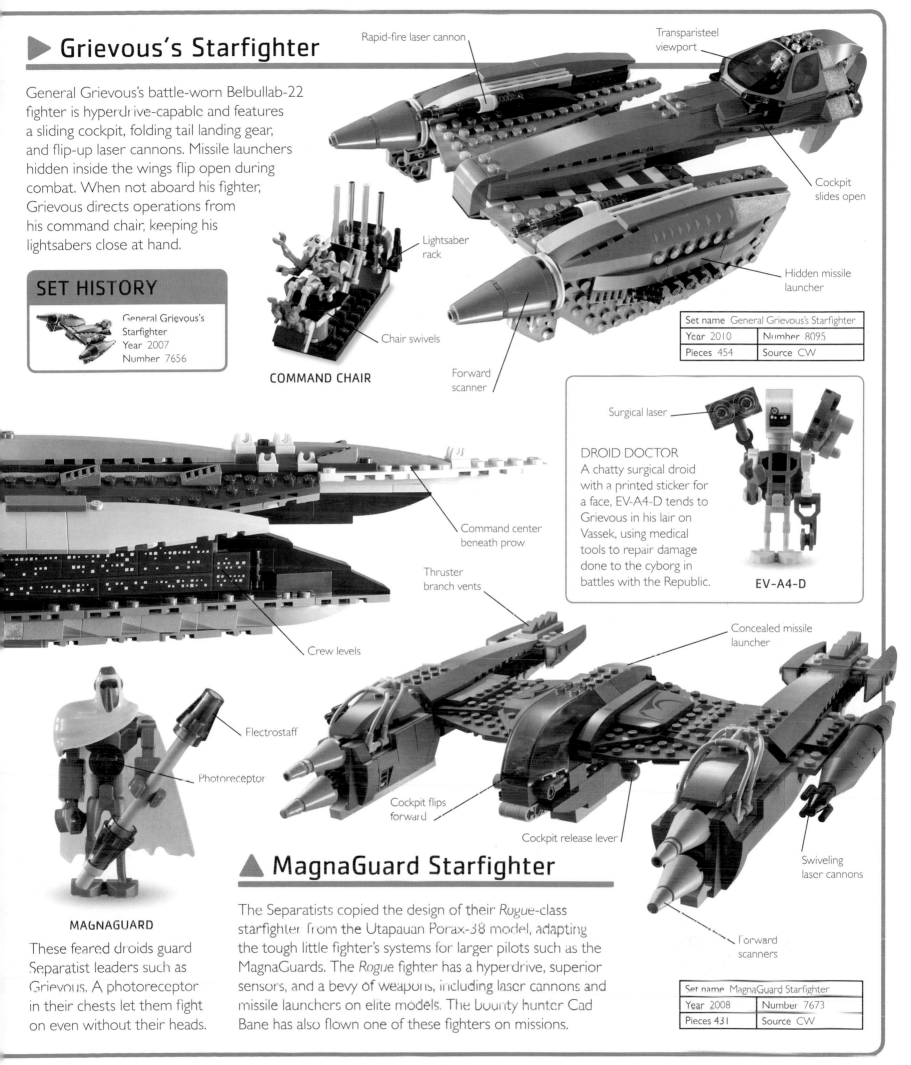

Rapid-fire laser cannon

Transparisteel viewport

Cockpit slides open

Hidden missile launcher

Lightsaber rack

Chair swivels

COMMAND CHAIR

Forward scanner

SET HISTORY

General Grievous's Starfighter
Year 2007
Number 7656

Set name	General Grievous's Starfighter	
Year 2010	Number	8095
Pieces 454	Source	CW

Command center beneath prow

Crew levels

Thruster branch vents

Surgical laser

DROID DOCTOR
A chatty surgical droid with a printed sticker for a face, EV-A4-D tends to Grievous in his lair on Vassek, using medical tools to repair damage done to the cyborg in battles with the Republic.

EV-A4-D

Concealed missile launcher

Electrostaff

Photoreceptor

Cockpit flips forward

Cockpit release lever

Swiveling laser cannons

Forward scanners

MAGNAGUARD

These feared droids guard Separatist leaders such as Grievous. A photoreceptor in their chests let them fight on even without their heads.

MagnaGuard Starfighter

The Separatists copied the design of their *Rogue*-class starfighter from the Utapauan Porax-38 model, adapting the tough little fighter's systems for larger pilots such as the MagnaGuards. The *Rogue* fighter has a hyperdrive, superior sensors, and a bevy of weapons, including laser cannons and missile launchers on elite models. The bounty hunter Cad Bane has also flown one of these fighters on missions.

Set name	MagnaGuard Starfighter	
Year 2008	Number	7673
Pieces 431	Source	CW

Geonosians

During the Clone Wars, the hive-dwelling Geonosians are notorious for their huge factories that endlessly churn out battle droids for the Separatist Army. A winged elite class rules over this savage, caste-based society, with wingless drones doing all the work. Geonosian soldiers carry exotic sonic weapons and fly twin-pronged fighter ships.

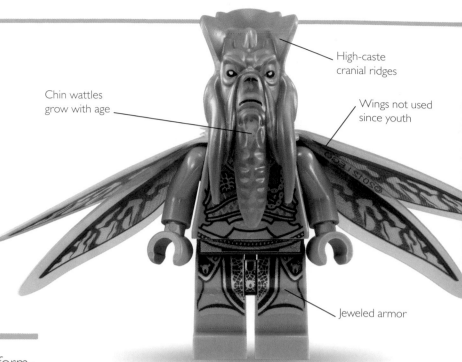

Chin wattles grow with age

High-caste cranial ridges

Wings not used since youth

Jeweled armor

▼ Geonosian Cannon

Geonosian soldiers deploy both handheld sonic blasters and platform-mounted sonic cannons, which fire balls of high-impact concussive energy. The LR1K cannon is a scaled-up artillery version of the handheld sonic blaster used by Geonosian drones belonging to the soldier caste. The cannon fires a sphere of sonic energy contained by a plasma charge. When the sphere hits its target, the plasma charge dissipates, releasing a devastating wave of sound. The cannon's platform can tilt up and down.

▲ Poggle the Lesser

A key Separatist leader, Poggle the Lesser takes his orders from Karina the Great, the hidden Queen of Geonosis who dwells in a subterranean lair. Poggle's minifigure, with its impressive quadruple wings, appears in the Duel on Geonosis (set 75017) from 2013.

Set name	Geonosian Cannon	
Year	2012	Number 9491
Pieces	132	Source CW

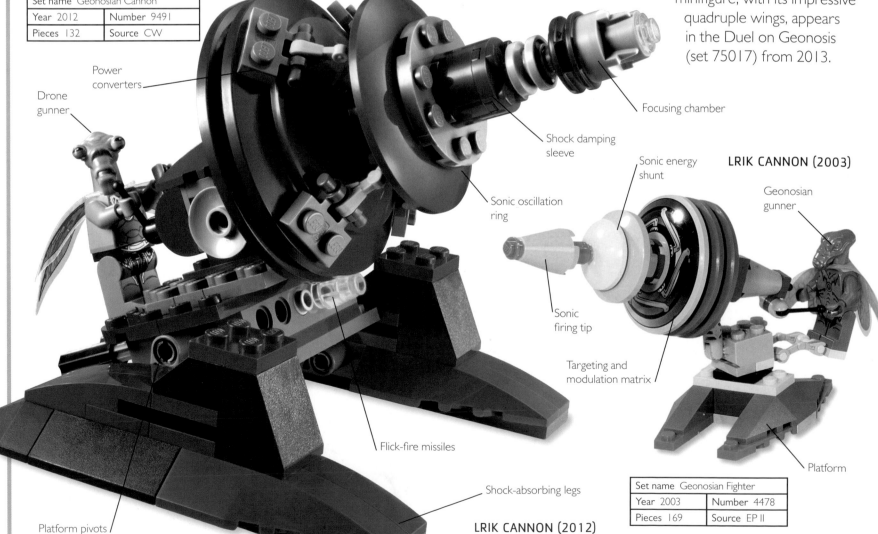

Power converters

Drone gunner

Focusing chamber

Shock damping sleeve

Sonic oscillation ring

LR1K CANNON (2003)

Sonic energy shunt

Geonosian gunner

Sonic firing tip

Targeting and modulation matrix

Flick-fire missiles

Platform

Shock-absorbing legs

Set name	Geonosian Fighter	
Year	2003	Number 4478
Pieces	169	Source EP II

Platform pivots

LR1K CANNON (2012)

46

▼ Geonosian Fighter

Thousands of deadly *Nantex*-class starfighters are launched against Republic forces at the Battle of Geonosis. These ships are specially designed to accommodate the anatomy of Geonosian pilots, and include a lifting cockpit hatch, swiveling laser cannon, and a hidden proton torpedo.

Set name	Geonosian Starfighter	
Year 2011	Number	7959
Pieces	155	Source CW

GEONOSIAN BATTLE DROIDS

The Geonosians designed the Separatists' battle droids as robot versions of themselves. These reddish-brown variants are camouflaged for battle on the desert surface of Geonosis.

GEONOSIAN BATTLE DROID

GEONOSIAN COMMANDER

Cockpit hatch opens for pilot access

Dorsal capacitor housing

Engine orb

Dorsal prong

Turret orb-mounted laser cannon

Gun-turret housing

BRICK FACTS

The Geonosian Fighter set was issued in 2003 in a black-themed box and again in 2004 in a blue box.

Detailed printing on torso

Disintegrated wings

Wings of soldier caste

Sonic blaster

GEONOSIAN PILOT

Ironically, Geonosian pilots lack wings. They receive orders through scent messages pumped into their star fighters' cockpits. The 2003 minifigure was dark gray; this 2011 redesign is light brown.

GEONOSIAN ZOMBIE

"Zombie" soldiers (actually exoskeletons controlled by brain-worm parasites) are captured in LEGO form by being muted gray and having tattered wings.

GEONOSIAN WARRIOR

Only Geonosian soldiers have functional wings. This 2012 minifigure, from the Geonosian Cannon set (9491), offers a more detailed head mold than its 2003 predecessor.

Naboo and Gungans

It takes an invasion by the villainous Trade Federation to propel peaceful Naboo to consider war. Its inhabitants—human Naboo and amphibious Gungans—must band together and work with their Jedi protectors to repel the hordes of merciless battle droids.

Set name	Gungan Patrol	
Year	2000	Number 7115
Pieces	77	Source EP1

Feathers indicate status

Energy shield

Jar Jar Binks

Battle wagon

Billed snout

Saddle made of fambaa skin

Energy ball

▲ Gungan Patrol

Gungans ride large, flightless kaadu. These amphibious animals are fast and agile. Many kaadu are used as beasts of burden, though larger four-legged falumpasets are also popular. These two kaadu, ridden by Jar Jar Binks and a Gungan soldier, pull wagons carrying energy-ball ammunition into battle against the droid army. The energy balls roll out of the back of the wagon.

▼ Naboo Swamp

Jedi Qui-Gon Jinn and Obi-Wan Kenobi land on Naboo to help its inhabitants. In the Naboo swamp, Qui-Gon Jinn uses his lightsaber to deflect blaster fire from battle droids on STAPs (Single Trooper Aerial Platforms) and shield his Gungan guide, Jar Jar Binks. The STAPs come with "invisible" stands to make them hover.

Set name	Naboo Swamp	
Year	1999	Number 7121
Pieces	81	Source EP1

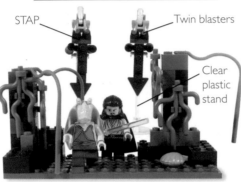

STAP

Twin blasters

Clear plastic stand

SET HISTORY

Gungan Sub
Year 1999
Number 7161

Set name	Gungan Sub	
Year	2012	Number 9499
Pieces	465	Film EP1

Underwater mine

Rotating drive fins

Detachable mini-sub

Cargo container

Forward cockpit bubble

Forward diving plane

▲ Gungan Sub

Qui-Gon, Obi-Wan, and Jar Jar Binks travel to Theed from the underwater city of Otoh Gunga in a bongo, or Gungan sub. Naboo's watery depths are home to dangerous monsters. The 2012 set has bongo defenses not shown onscreen: a mine to scare off attackers, flick-fire missiles, and a detachable mini-sub for a quick getaway. It was also the first LEGO set to feature a Queen Amidala minifigure in all her royal garb.

▼ Flash Speeder

A Naboo security officer pilots a repulsorlift flash speeder: one of the ground craft used for patrols in peacetime, but employed in the defense of Theed Palace during the invasion of Naboo.

Set name	Flash Speeder	
Year	2000	Number 7124
Pieces	105	Source EP1

Blaster (secret compartment beneath)

Twin-seat model

Wing-mounted engines

◀ Jar Jar Binks

A good-hearted but clumsy exile from Otoh Gunga, Jar Jar rises from humble beginnings to help represent Naboo in the Galactic Senate. Back in 1999, his minifigure was the first to have a unique headsculpt. Printing was added to the mold in 2011.

Umbarans and Mandalorians

The Republic faces many perils in the galaxy's Outer Rim as the Clone Wars grind on. The shadowy world of Umbara is home to Separatist-allied soldiers whose technology rivals anything in the Republic. Mandalore is a neutral world, but ruthless warriors known as the Death Watch will stop at nothing to overthrow its ruler, the pacifist Duchess Satine.

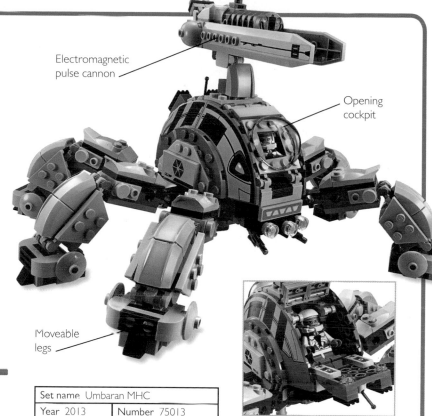

Electromagnetic pulse cannon

Opening cockpit

Moveable legs

Set name	Umbaran MHC	
Year	2013	Number 75013
Pieces	493	Source CW

REAR COCKPIT

▼ The Death Watch

Duchess Satine insists Mandalore has left its warlike past behind. But a secretive band of armored warriors, the Death Watch, has allied itself with the Separatists. Well-armed and deadly, they seek to take over the planet.

SPEEDER

Set name	Mandalorian Battle Pack	
Year	2011	Number 7914
Pieces	68	Source CW

Sniper rifle

MANDALORIAN ASSASSIN

Swiveling cannon

GUN TURRET

▲ Umbaran Cannon

On Umbara, one of the toughest opponents for the clones is the juggernaut or Mobile Heavy Cannon. A blast from this six-legged tank can wipe out an entire Republic platoon. This 2013 Umbaran MHC comes with Ahsoka Tano, a 212th Attack Battalion clone trooper, and two Umbaran soldiers.

UMBARAN SOLDIER

MANDALORIANS
Death Watch's Mandalorian supercommandos are led by Pre Vizsla, who wields the Darksaber: an ancient lightsaber with a black blade. After Darth Maul takes over Death Watch, the supercommandos repaint their armor red and black in his honor.

Maul's colors

Darksaber

MANDALORIAN SUPERCOMMANDO

PRE VIZSLA

▼ Mandalorian Speeder

When Maul and Death Watch take over Mandalore, they patrol its skies in these fast, powerful police speeders. The craft is full of surprises: Its front hatch hides a missile emplacement, while its gun turret is built atop a secret weapons locker.

Elevating cannon

Hidden weapons locker

Missiles hidden beneath hatch

Weapons rack

Armored skirt

Set name	Mandalorian Speeder	
Year	2013	Number 75022
Pieces	211	Source CW

Bounty Hunters

Bounty hunters track down and capture people in order to collect a fee, or bounty. These ruthless, capable hunters prefer to work alone, but occasionally they hire fellow professionals such as assassin Zam Wesell. Two of the most legendary bounty hunters in the galaxy are Jango Fett and his son, Boba Fett.

▶ Jango Fett's *Slave I*

Jango Fett's *Firespray*-class patrol and attack ship, *Slave I*, is bristling with weapons, many of which are hidden in order to deliver devastating surprise assaults. The armaments consist of two four-barrel foldout blaster cannons, twin rotating laser cannons, two concealed heat-seeking rocket launchers, and three drop-bombs, as well as a removable prisoner cage. A smuggling box can be magnetically attached to the underside of the ship. When the repulsorlift wings swivel, they rotate the cockpit from landing to flight mode.

Set name	Jango Fett's *Slave I*	
Year 2002	Number 7153	
Pieces 358	Source EP II & V	

Twin blaster cannons

Repulsorlift wing

JANGO FETT

Dented helmet

BOBA FETT

Rangefinder

JANGO'S SON
Jango Fett treats Boba as his son, but the boy is actually an unaltered clone whom Jango teaches to be a bounty hunter. The 2013 Advent Calendar (set 75023) introduced a young Boba with natural skin tones.

YOUNG BOBA

EE-3 blaster

▶ Boba Fett

The adult Boba Fett from Desert Skiff (set 9496) is the most detailed Fett yet, featuring repainted Mandalorian armor, a helmet and jetpack, a swiveling rangefinder and a cape. Very rare bronze, silver, and gold Fetts were offered as prizes at conventions.

▶ Boba Fett's *Slave I*

Boba Fett inherits *Slave I* from his father, Jango. He has added modifications of his own, including several upgraded weapons systems. The 2010 set features an opening cargo bay, a cockpit, and wings that automatically rotate into flight mode. Close attention also reveals concealed spring-loaded cannons, a hidden missile carousel, and swiveling short-range twin blasters on the tail.

Set name	*Slave I*	
Year 2010	Number 8097	
Pieces 573	Source EP IV & VI	

Cockpit viewscreen

Concealed missile carousel

Sensor array

Armor plating

Wing strut

Wing extension strut

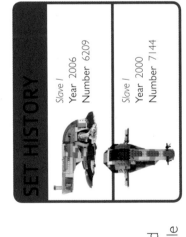

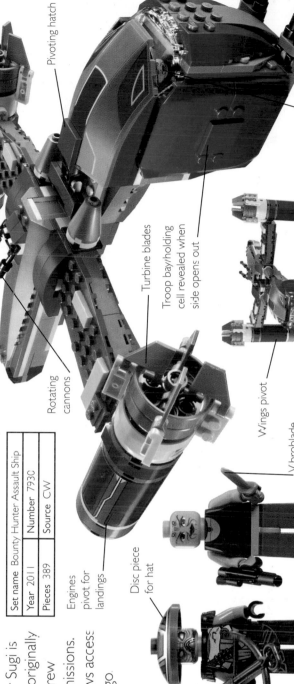

GALACTIC ROGUES

After the Battle of Hoth, Darth Vader hired bounty hunters to pursue the *Millennium Falcon*. Among those answering his call were Fett, the Trandoshan Bossk, the scarred human called Dengar, and the assassin droid IG-88.

IG-88

Bandages

DENGAR

Flight suit

BOSSK

ZAM WESELL

▼ Zam Wesell's Airspeeder

Hired assassin Zam Wesell flies an airspeeder for quick getaways on risky missions. It is streamlined and fast, which makes it difficult for Anakin and Obi-Wan to give chase in a borrowed airspeeder through the towering spires of Coruscant. Zam's cockpit screen is hinged and a hidden mechanism makes the wings fall off, re-creating the crash-landing at the end of the high-speed chase in the movie.

Set name	Bounty Hunter Pursuit	
Year 2002	Number 7133	
Pieces 259	Source EP II	

Cockpit

Front mandible

Storage compartment

Aerodynamic tail fin

Heat dispersal tip

Cockpit door

CARGO HATCH

Blaster cannons

Hidden laser cannon

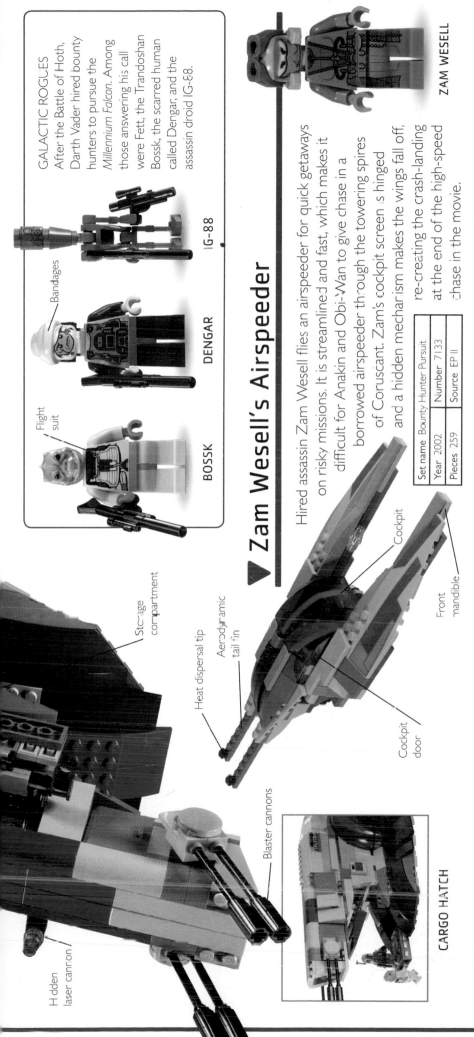

▲ Bounty Hunter Assault Ship

During the Clone Wars, the Zabrak bounty hunter Sugi is captain of a gunship called the *Halo*. The craft was originally built for military strikes, but Sugi refitted it with a crew cabin and hold, making it suitable for longer-term missions. Sliding the top of the hull pivots the wings and allows access to a hidden compartment for stashing valuable cargo

GUNS FOR HIRE

Most bounty hunters are loyal only to money, taking on any job that promises a profit. After Jango's death, the ruthless Aurra Sing continues Boba Fett's education as a hunter. These three LEGO minifigures are exclusive to the Bounty Hunter Assault Ship (set 7930).

Set name	Bounty Hunter Assault Ship	
Year 2011	Number 7930	
Pieces 389	Source CW	

Pivoting hatch

Sugi in crew cabin

Turbine blades

Troop bay/holding cell revealed when side opens out

Wings pivot

Vibroblade

LANDING MODE

Rotating cannons

Engines pivot for landings

Disc piece for hat

SUGI

Bowcaster

EMBO

AURRA SING

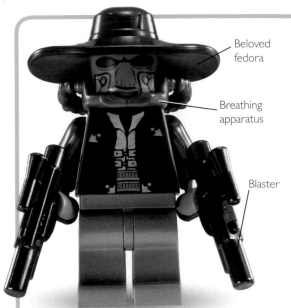

Beloved fedora

Breathing apparatus

Blaster

CAD BANE

A Duros bounty hunter, Cad Bane is infamous across the galaxy for his ruthlessness and successfull methods. He often works for the Sith Lord Darth Sidious.

SECRET MISSILES

Cad Bane

The breakdown in order during the Clone Wars allows the galactic underworld to thrive. Amoral bounty hunters such as Cad Bane sell their services to the highest bidder, stealing, kidnapping, and raiding on behalf of anyone who has the credits to buy their short-lived loyalty. Pirate gangs such as the one led by Hondo Ohnaka ambush travelers and attack ships with little fear that law enforcement will interfere with their illegal activities.

Set name	Cad Bane's Speeder	
Year	2010	Number 8128
Pieces	318	Source CW

Bow hatch

Headlights hide missiles

Storage compartment

Cybernetic arm

SHAHAN ALAMA

Enlisted by Cad Bane to join his group of bandits, Shahan Alama wears a red beret—a nod to his previous life as a pirate.

▼ Cad Bane's Speeder

Cad Bane and his crew favor these repulsorlift vehicles for their high speeds and agility. In one of his most daring raids, Bane and a gang of hired thugs attack the Senate Building in the heart of Coruscant, taking a group of Senators hostage and demanding that the Republic free crime lord Ziro the Hutt in exchange for the captives. Bane and his hunters, including Shahan Alama and an assassin droid, then flee the Senate.

FELLOW OUTLAWS

Led by Hondo Ohnaka, Weequay pirates on the planet Florrum use spaceships, speeder bikes, and tanks to defend their base. For ground operations, Hondo depends on his WLO-5 tanks, which boast thick armor and heavy guns. "Speak softly and drive a big tank," as the pirate boss likes to say.

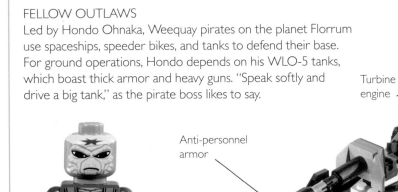

Fancy stolen coat

Turbine engine

Anti-personnel armor

Ancient pistols

Pop-up mechanism opens hatch doors

Steering vane

TURK FALSO

Missile launcher

Set name	Pirate Tank	
Year	2009	Number 7753
Pieces	372	Source CW

HONDO OHNAKA

Hondo Ohnaka believes in grog, loot, and good times, though he is not without a sense of honor. He shares his black epaulets with the bounty hunter Embo and a LEGO space officer.

HH-87 Starhopper

HH-87 Starhoppers are tough little gunships favored by lawless organizations in the shadowy corners of the galaxy, such as Zygerrian slavers, pirates, and the Hutt clans. While on the Hutt homeworld of Nal Hutta, HH-87s piloted by Hutt servants hunt down a ship carrying the bounty hunter Cad Bane, who has fled to Nal Hutta with a disguised Obi-Wan.

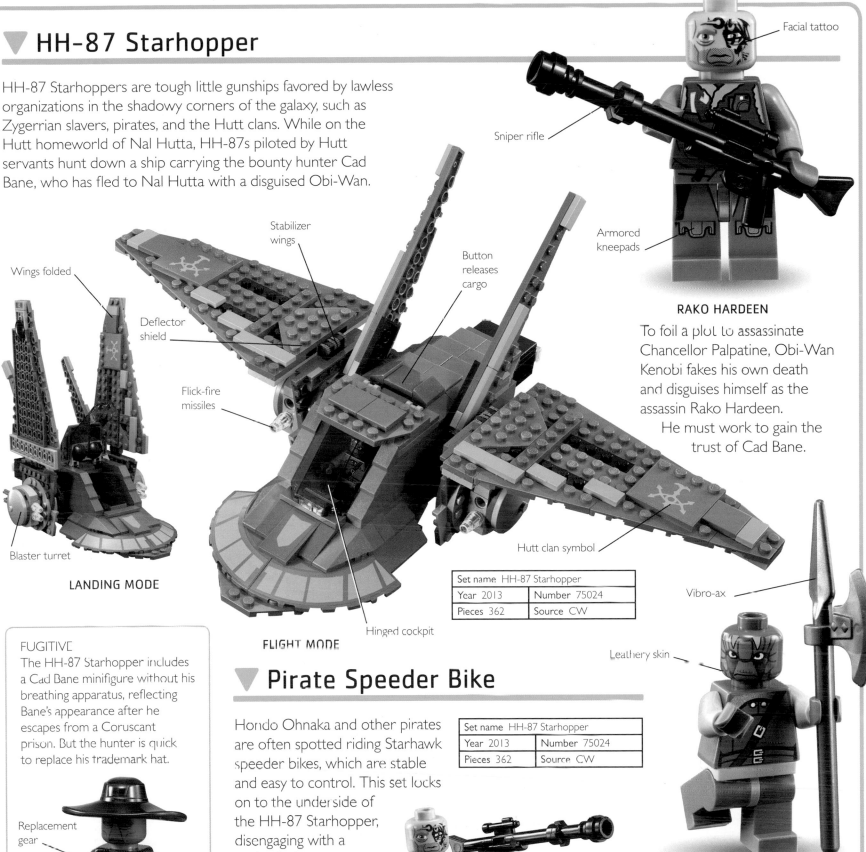

Facial tattoo

Sniper rifle

Armored kneepads

RAKO HARDEEN

To foil a plot to assassinate Chancellor Palpatine, Obi-Wan Kenobi fakes his own death and disguises himself as the assassin Rako Hardeen.
He must work to gain the trust of Cad Bane.

Wings folded

Deflector shield

Stabilizer wings

Button releases cargo

Flick-fire missiles

Blaster turret

LANDING MODE

Hutt clan symbol

Vibro-ax

Leathery skin

Set name	HH-87 Starhopper	
Year 2013	Number 75024	
Pieces 362	Source CW	

Hinged cockpit

FLIGHT MODE

FUGITIVE
The HH-87 Starhopper includes a Cad Bane minifigure without his breathing apparatus, reflecting Bane's appearance after he escapes from a Coruscant prison. But the hunter is quick to replace his trademark hat.

Replacement gear

CAD BANE (WITHOUT BREATHING APPARATUS)

Pirate Speeder Bike

Hondo Ohnaka and other pirates are often spotted riding Starhawk speeder bikes, which are stable and easy to control. This set locks on to the underside of the HH-87 Starhopper, disengaging with a push of a button.

Set name	HH-87 Starhopper	
Year 2013	Number 75024	
Pieces 362	Source CW	

Attachment point

Control yoke

Front repulsorlift

Airscoop

NIKTO GUARD

The Hutts dislike manual labor, leaving such work to hirelings and servants of various species, such as the Nikto. These leathery-skinned aliens serve the Hutts as pilots and guards.

Anakin Skywalker —Fallen Jedi

Tormented by visions of Padmé Amidala coming to harm, Anakin turns to Chancellor Palpatine, who hints that there is more to the Force than Jedi teachings. He also reveals his true identity: He is the Sith Lord Darth Sidious! Desperate to save Padmé, Anakin falls to the dark side, leading Sidious's assault on the Jedi and crossing lightsabers with his old master Obi-Wan Kenobi on the lava planet Mustafar.

▼ Palpatine's Arrest

Mace Windu assembles a party of Jedi to arrest Chancellor Palpatine, but the Sith Lord proves full of tricks and his office has many surprises: Will Mace fall victim to the hidden locker of dark-side weapons, or get flung out of the set's breakaway window? Anakin docks his airspeeder and rushes into the fray, where he must choose between his loyalty to the Jedi and his hunger to learn the dark side's secrets.

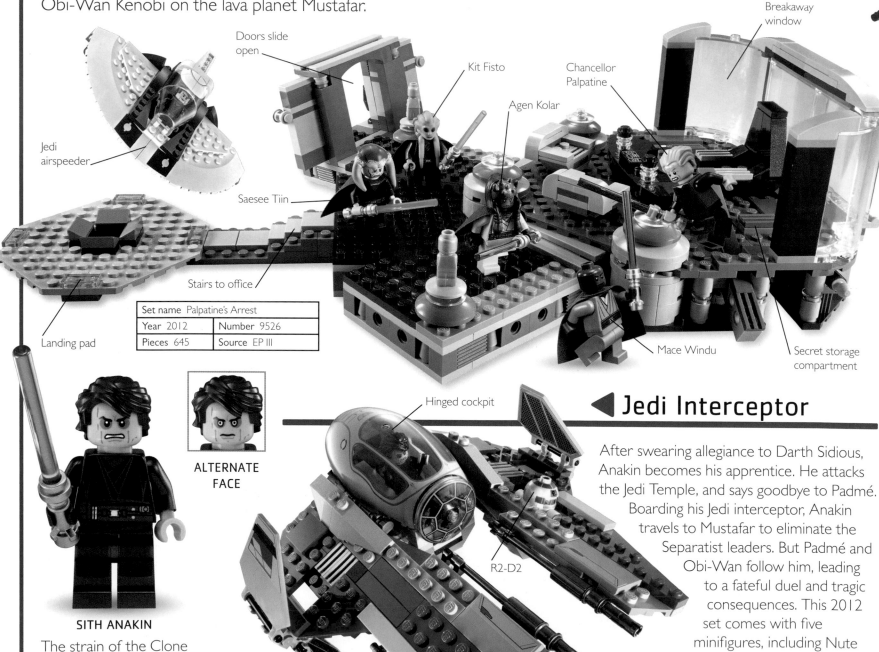

Doors slide open

Kit Fisto

Chancellor Palpatine

Breakaway window

Jedi airspeeder

Saesee Tiin

Agen Kolar

Stairs to office

Landing pad

Mace Windu

Secret storage compartment

Set name	Palpatine's Arrest	
Year	2012	Number 9526
Pieces	645	Source EP III

SITH ANAKIN

The strain of the Clone Wars shows on the face of Anakin's Episode III minifigure. His alternate face has yellow Sith eyes.

ALTERNATE FACE

Hinged cockpit

◀ Jedi Interceptor

After swearing allegiance to Darth Sidious, Anakin becomes his apprentice. He attacks the Jedi Temple, and says goodbye to Padmé. Boarding his Jedi interceptor, Anakin travels to Mustafar to eliminate the Separatist leaders. But Padmé and Obi-Wan follow him, leading to a fateful duel and tragic consequences. This 2012 set comes with five minifigures, including Nute Gunray and a battle droid.

R2-D2

Wings unfold in flight mode

Ion cannon

Laser cannons

Set name	Jedi Interceptor	
Year	2012	Number 9494
Pieces	300	Source EP III

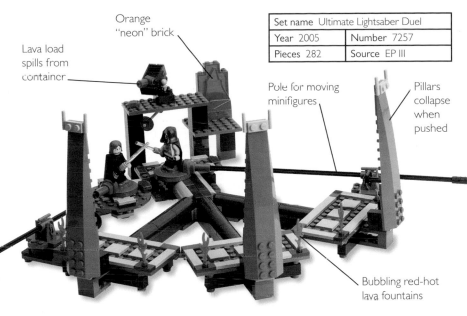

Lava load spills from container

Orange "neon" brick

Set name	Ultimate Lightsaber Duel	
Year 2005		Number 7257
Pieces 282		Source EP III

Pole for moving minifigures

Pillars collapse when pushed

Bubbling red-hot lava fountains

▲ Duel on Mustafar

Teetering on service platforms above the red-hot lava of Mustafar, Obi-Wan fights his former Padawan, Anakin Skywalker, now recruited to the Sith and renamed Darth Vader. They are moved on long rods and their lightsabers glow. Meanwhile the pillars could come crashing down at any time!

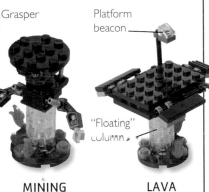

MINING PLANET Battling on Mustafar, Anakin and Obi-Wan seek safe places above the deadly lava. Their saber duel takes place atop confused mining droids and across repulsorlift platforms. These two come with Anakin's Jedi Interceptor (set 9494).

Grasper

Platform beacon

"Floating" column

MINING DROID

LAVA PLATFORM

▶ Obi-Wan

In the Jedi Temple, Obi-Wan discovers Anakin has betrayed the Jedi and pledged allegiance to the Sith. Heartbroken but determined to turn his old Padawan back to the light, Obi-Wan follows Anakin's Jedi Interceptor (set 9494) to Mustafar. This 2012 minifigure has an alternate, fierce face for displaying his determination to destroy this new threat to the galaxy.

▼ Battle-Damaged Anakin

The duel on Mustafar leaves Anakin terribly burned, as shown in the printed detail on the front and back of his torso, made specifically for this minifigure. Left for dead by a distraught Obi-Wan, he is rescued by Palpatine, who begins Anakin's transformation into Darth Vader, forever trapped in a mask and armor.

Set name	Emperor Palpatine's Shuttle	
Year 2010		Number 8096
Pieces 592		Source EP III

Sith lightsaber

SURGICAL TABLE

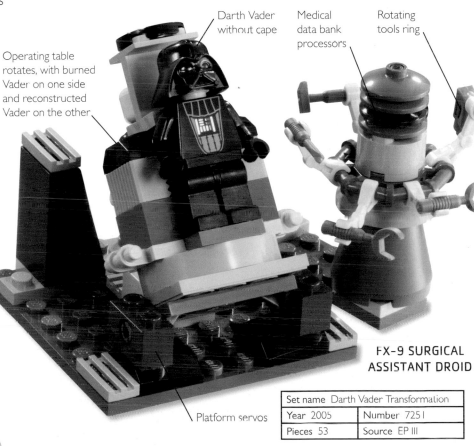

Darth Vader without cape

Medical data bank processors

Rotating tools ring

Operating table rotates, with burned Vader on one side and reconstructed Vader on the other

Platform servos

FX-9 SURGICAL ASSISTANT DROID

Set name	Darth Vader Transformation	
Year 2005		Number 7251
Pieces 53		Source EP III

▲ Rehabilitation Center

After his battle with Obi-Wan Kenobi on Mustafar, Vader would have died had Palpatine not taken him to a secret medcenter on Coruscant. A medical droid stabilizes Vader's burned body and organs, then encases him in a life-supporting black suit of armor.

Wookiees

During the Clone Wars, an epic battle takes place on Kashyyyk, home planet of the Wookiees. Droid armies face fierce resistance from well-armed and proud Wookiee warriors, led by the chieftain Tarfful and including Chewbacca. Wookiees use traditional wood-framed vehicles, many of which are unarmed, but the Wookiees' knowledge of the swamps and forests of their planet gives them an advantage over the ruthless droids.

On Kashyyyk, Separatist battle droids, spider droids, and tank droids launch a massive attack. The Wookiees fight bravely in their ornithopters, catamarans, and other vehicles, supported by Republic clone troops led by Jedi generals.

◀ Ornithopter

Wookiee ornithopters, also known as fluttercraft, are lightweight, two-seated fliers used to patrol the swamps of Kashyyyk. During the Battle of Kashyyyk, Wookiee pilots and gunners fly these open-cockpit craft, many retrofitted with tail-mounted laser cannons, relying on speed and agility to avoid incoming fire.

Radiator grille

Pressure release vents

Laser cannon tail-gun

Maneuverable flight wings

Power generator

Wooden framework

Primary control nexus

Set name Wookiee Attack	
Year 2005	Number 7258
Pieces 537	Source EP III

Steering vanes

Stabilizing flaps

CLONE LEADER
Like the 41st Elite Corps troopers he commands, Gree's 2014 minifigure is dirty and battle-scarred. This seasoned clone leader carries a blaster weapon and specialist macrobinoculars.

CLONE COMMANDER GREE

▶ Kashyyyk Troopers

Camouflaged to blend in on lush, jungle planets, the 41st Elite Corps come to the Wookiees' defense on Kashyyyk. The troopers' minifigure armor is printed to look scratched and battle-worn after lengthy duty in hostile terrains.

Phase II helmet

Blaster propels stud

Scout trooper helmet

KASHYYYK CLONE TROOPER

41ST ELITE CORPS TROOPER

Kashyyyk long-gun

Clan pectoral

WOOKIEE WARRIOR
An old friend of Chewbacca's, the clan chieftain Tarfful fights alongside the Republic's clones on Kashyyyk. Then he helps rescue Yoda when the clone troopers mysteriously turn their guns on their Jedi generals. Tarfful fights with a long-barreled rifle and wears a bandolier displaying his clan emblem on a pectoral.

CHIEF TARFFUL

▼ Catamaran

Slim, twin-hulled Wookiee catamarans skim over the waters of Kashyyyk at great speeds. During the Battle of Kashyyyk, Chewbacca joins forces with Yoda and Luminara Unduli on board a catamaran to make a raid on Separatist lines. Usually unarmed, this retrofitted catamaran features a centrally mounted heavy missile cannon and several bombs (dropped from each hull). Catamarans are lifted by repulsors and propelled by jet engines or, as here, propeller pods.

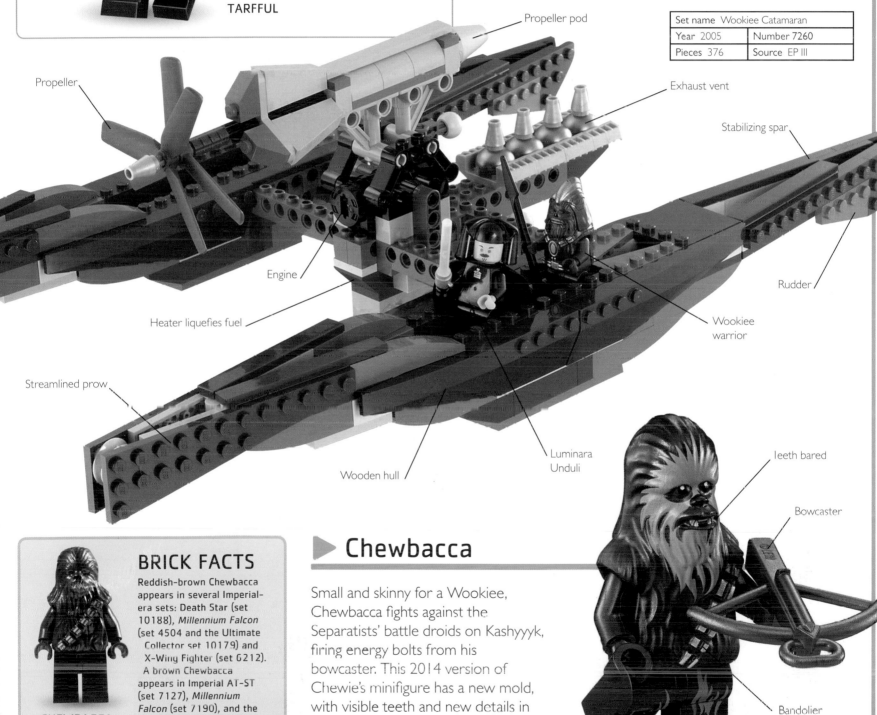

Propeller pod

Propeller

Exhaust vent

Stabilizing spar

Engine

Heater liquefies fuel

Rudder

Wookiee warrior

Streamlined prow

Wooden hull

Luminara Unduli

Set name	Wookiee Catamaran	
Year	2005	Number 7260
Pieces	376	Source EP III

Teeth bared

Bowcaster

▶ Chewbacca

Small and skinny for a Wookiee, Chewbacca fights against the Separatists' battle droids on Kashyyyk, firing energy bolts from his bowcaster. This 2014 version of Chewie's minifigure has a new mold, with visible teeth and new details in his multicolored fur and eyes. His bowcaster is now black. He's found in Droid Gunship (set 75042).

Bandolier

BRICK FACTS
Reddish-brown Chewbacca appears in several Imperial-era sets: Death Star (set 10188), *Millennium Falcon* (set 4504 and the Ultimate Collector set 10179) and X-Wing Fighter (set 6212). A brown Chewbacca appears in Imperial AT-ST (set 7127), *Millennium Falcon* (set 7190), and the minifigure pack, Star Wars #3 (set 3342).

CHEWBACCA (REDDISH-BROWN)

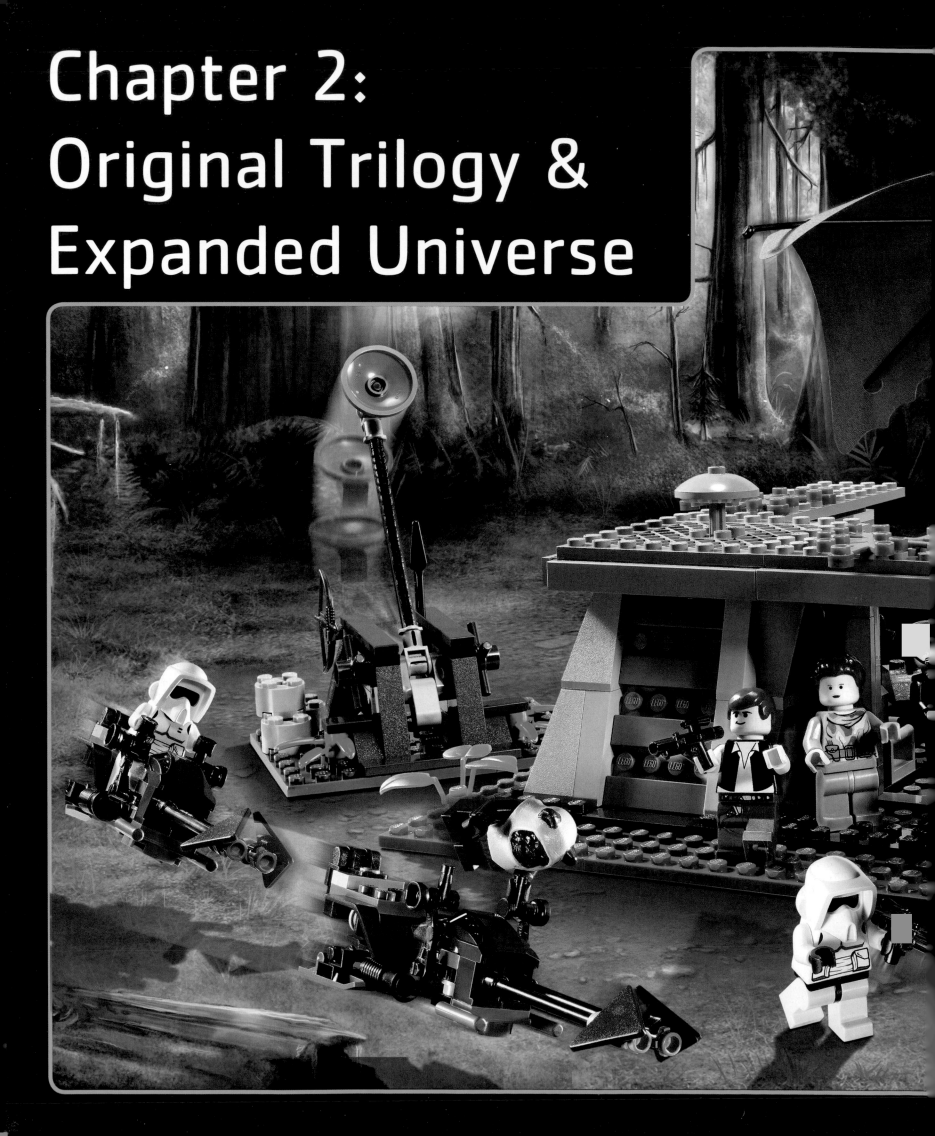

Chapter 2:
Original Trilogy &
Expanded Universe

Luke Skywalker

Yearning for adventure, farm boy Luke Skywalker grows up on a remote planet named Tatooine. When he meets Obi-Wan Kenobi, Luke begins to learn the truth of his origins as the secret son of Anakin Skywalker. Luke's journey transforms him into a pilot for the Rebel Alliance and a Jedi Knight—and ends in a reconciliation with his father and freedom from Imperial rule for the galaxy.

▶ T-16 Skyhopper

With the demise of Podracing on Tatooine, teenagers take to racing skyhoppers through narrow ravines, blasting womp rats with front-mounted rifles. Luke owns an Incom T-16 skyhopper (though his Uncle Owen disapproves of it). This variant model features an open cockpit (standard models feature a pressurized cabin for sub-orbital travel). A compartment in the upper airfoil holds the electrobinoculars and blaster included with the set.

Upper airfoil

Pilot in open cockpit

Flying decal

Wing-mounted cannon

Set name	T-16 Skyhopper	
Year 2003	Number 4477	
Pieces 96	Source EP IV & VI	

Heavy-duty gun

Movable lower airfoil

▼ Luke's Landspeeder

Set name	Cantina	
Year 2014	Number 75052	
Pieces 615	Source EP IV	

Luke and his new friends travel around the desert terrain of his homeworld in his battered X-34 landspeeder. Its low-power repulsors make it hover off the ground, while triple turbines provide thrust. Speeders are a common sight on Tatooine, though heat and sand make maintenance a constant headache.

Dorsal turbine hides secret compartment

Obi-Wan Kenobi

SET HISTORY

Luke's Landspeeder
Year 2010
Number 8092

Mos Eisley Cantina
Year 2004
Number 4501

Landspeeder
Year 1999
Number 7110

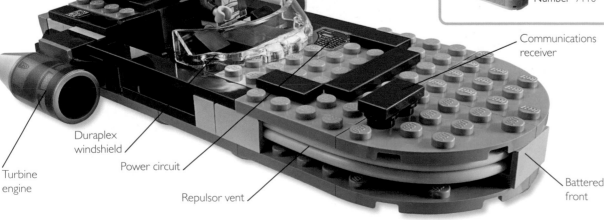

Turbine engine

Duraplex windshield

Power circuit

Repulsor vent

Communications receiver

Battered front

LUKE ON TATOOINE

On the desolate planet Tatooine, Luke wears a simple farm tunic, a utility belt for his tools, and leg bindings to keep out the planet's sand.

▼ X-Wing Starfighter

SET HISTORY

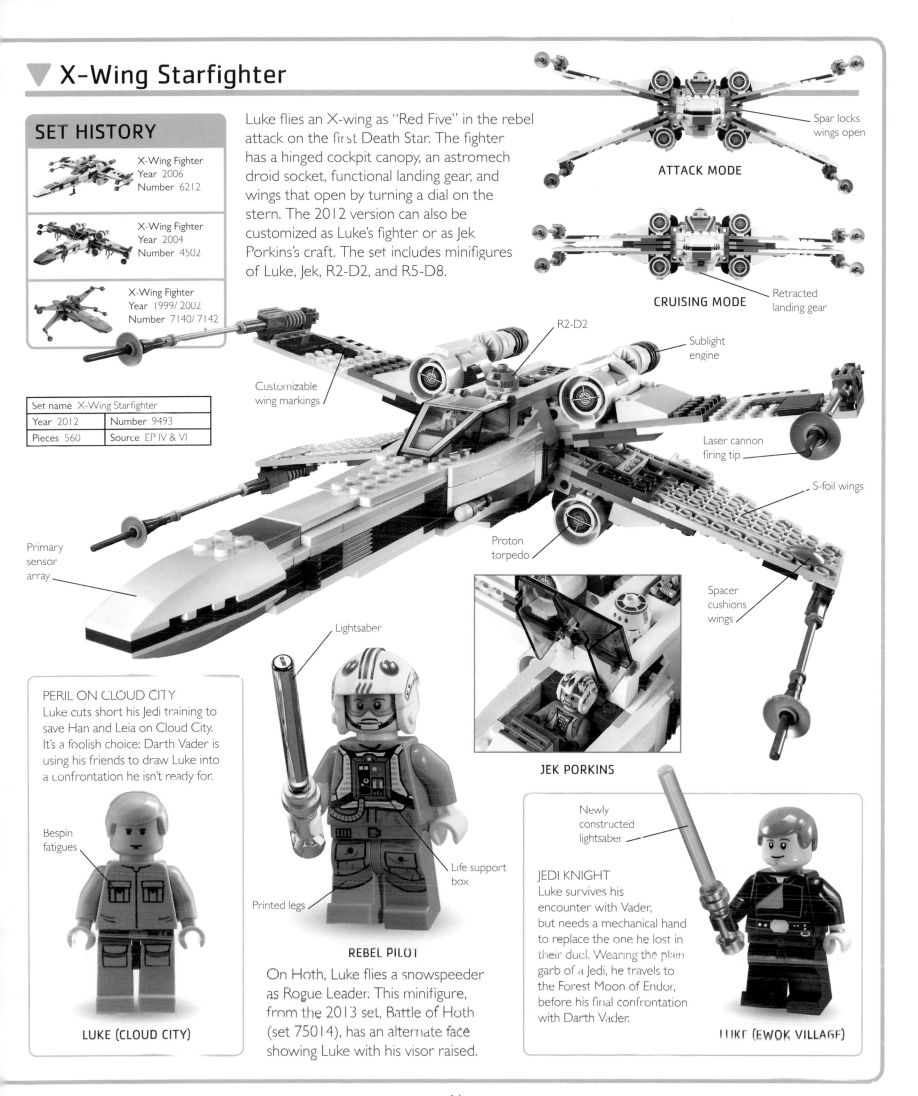

	X-Wing Fighter Year 2006 Number 6212
	X-Wing Fighter Year 2004 Number 4502
	X-Wing Fighter Year 1999/ 2002 Number 7140/ 7142

Luke flies an X-wing as "Red Five" in the rebel attack on the first Death Star. The fighter has a hinged cockpit canopy, an astromech droid socket, functional landing gear, and wings that open by turning a dial on the stern. The 2012 version can also be customized as Luke's fighter or as Jek Porkins's craft. The set includes minifigures of Luke, Jek, R2-D2, and R5-D8.

Spar locks wings open

ATTACK MODE

Retracted landing gear

CRUISING MODE

Set name	X-Wing Starfighter	
Year 2012	Number 9493	
Pieces 560	Source EP IV & VI	

Customizable wing markings

R2-D2

Sublight engine

Laser cannon firing tip

S-foil wings

Primary sensor array

Proton torpedo

Spacer cushions wings

JEK PORKINS

Lightsaber

PERIL ON CLOUD CITY
Luke cuts short his Jedi training to save Han and Leia on Cloud City. It's a foolish choice: Darth Vader is using his friends to draw Luke into a confrontation he isn't ready for.

Bespin fatigues

Life support box

Printed legs

LUKE (CLOUD CITY)

REBEL PILOT

On Hoth, Luke flies a snowspeeder as Rogue Leader. This minifigure, from the 2013 set, Battle of Hoth (set 75014), has an alternate face showing Luke with his visor raised.

Newly constructed lightsaber

JEDI KNIGHT
Luke survives his encounter with Vader, but needs a mechanical hand to replace the one he lost in their duel. Wearing the plain garb of a Jedi, he travels to the Forest Moon of Endor, before his final confrontation with Darth Vader.

LUKE (EWOK VILLAGE)

Escape Pod

C-3PO and R2-D2 slip into a small escape pod to avoid being caught by Darth Vader when he seizes the rebel blockade runner. After the droids crash-land on Tatooine, Jawas capture them and sell them to Owen Lars.

Set name	Droid Escape	
Year 2012	Number 9490	
Pieces 137	Source EP IV	

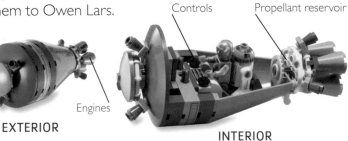

Controls

Propellant reservoir

Engines

EXTERIOR

INTERIOR

Cockpit

JAWA

A Jawa steers the sandcrawler from inside the cockpit, situated high on the front of the vehicle. It is hinged at the top for access.

DROID CARGO
The other droids in the sandcrawler are: A GNK power droid; a WED Treadwell repair droid; a faulty astromech, R5-D4; an R2 unit droid; and an R1-series droid refitted with the armored shell of a Mark II reactor drone.

Optical sensors

GONK DROID

WED TREADWELL DROID

R5-D4

R2 UNIT

R1-SERIES DROID

Sandcrawler

On Tatooine, Jawas patrol the deserts and wastelands in large sandcrawlers in search of salvage from spaceship crashes. Sandcrawlers are forgotten relics from the days when Tatooine was a mining colony. Jawas have repurposed them to round up stray droids, old vehicles, and scrap metal or minerals that can be used or sold. Each sandcrawler is home to an entire clan of Jawas, and serves as transport, workshop, traveling store—and protection from desert predators or rampaging Sand People.

Mobile Junkyard

In the workshop, Jawas use scrap parts to mend broken equipment or droids. After a sale, the Jawas move on quickly, as their patched-up goods rarely remain working for long.

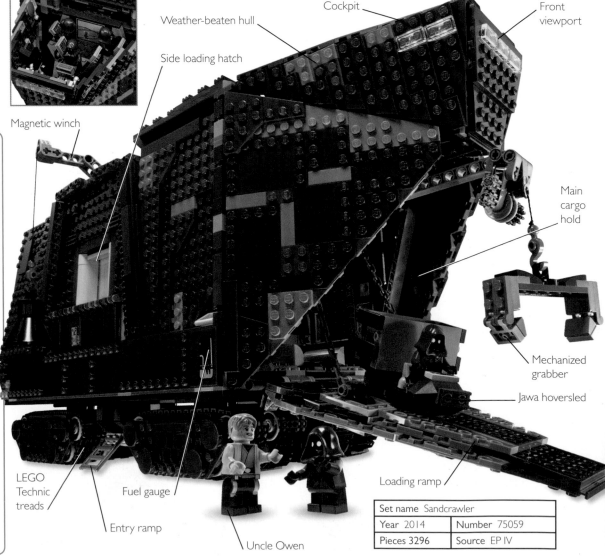

Weather-beaten hull

Cockpit

Front viewport

Side loading hatch

Magnetic winch

Main cargo hold

Mechanized grabber

Jawa hoversled

LEGO Technic treads

Fuel gauge

Loading ramp

Entry ramp

Uncle Owen

Set name	Sandcrawler	
Year 2014	Number 75059	
Pieces 3296	Source EP IV	

Jedi in Hiding

After swearing allegiance to the Sith, Anakin Skywalker helps Darth Sidious hunt down the Jedi and turn the Republic into the Galactic Empire. The few Jedi who survive become refugees, hoping to avoid detection by Darth Vader and his Emperor. Obi-Wan Kenobi gives the infant Luke Skywalker to the Lars family on Tatooine and dwells in the desert, while Yoda hides on a little-known planet in the Outer Rim.

▼ Yoda's Hut

Yoda survives the Great Jedi Purge at the end of the Clone Wars to live in exile on Dagobah. He lands on the planet in an escape pod, which he makes into a hut. Yoda's lifestyle on the swamp planet is frugal: his dwelling is furnished with a simple bed, table, cooking pot, and barrels.

Set name	X-Wing Fighter	
Year	2004	Number 4502
Pieces	563	Source EP V & VI

Entrance

Native Dagobah foliage

EXTERIOR

Hut dome

Yoda's bed

Stove

INTERIOR

MASTER IN DISGUISE

Yoda carries a gnarled gimer stick, but for proof of his Jedi satus, lift his bed to find his secret lightsaber.

Luke carries Yoda when training

JEDI IN TRAINING

When Luke is training with Yoda, he wears a sleeveless green shirt, gray pants, and a green backpack.

YODA (WHITE HAIR)

Eight hundred years of life have taught Yoda patience, and changed his appearance. This is the third incarnation of Yoda—the updated minifigure is based on the *Star Wars: Clone Wars* TV series and features a new white hair pattern on the back of his head.

Gray hair

Jedi robes

BEN KENOBI (JEDI MASTER)

Obi-Wan's exile comes to an end when he receives a distress call from Princess Leia. He puts on his Jedi cloak and hood to lead Luke on a rescue mission.

BEN KENOBI (TATOOINE)

In exile on Tatooine, Obi-Wan becomes known as "Ben Kenobi". He keeps a quiet watch over Luke, Anakin's son, waiting for the day he can teach him about the Force.

Han Solo and Chewbacca

He's a rogue and a scoundrel. Worst of all, according to Princess Leia, he's scruffy-looking. But Han Solo and copilot Chewbacca fly one of the fastest ships in the galaxy. The *Millennium Falcon* is also scruffy-looking, but, according to Solo, it "made the Kessel Run in less than 12 parsecs." The ship needs to be smart and fast: Solo has a bounty on his head for unpaid debts to Jabba the Hutt. What a time to get mixed up in a rebellion against the Empire!

YOUNG HAN

WHO'S IAN?
The 2011 animated LEGO feature *The Padawan Menace* introduced Ian, a fast-talking orphan who poses as a Jedi youngling before revealing his real name: Han. The Blu-ray DVD included an exclusive Young Han minifigure, with a cocky grin already in place.

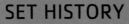

Vaporator antenna

Bar area

Concealed blaster for troublesome patrons

Hinged wall section

Panel with window from castle sets

Traditional Tatooine dome roof

Lever operates sliding door

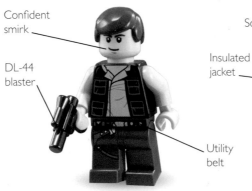

Han Solo with blaster at the ready

Greedo

Customer entrance

▲ Cantina

When one of Jabba the Hutt's minions, Greedo, accosts Han Solo in the Mos Eisley Cantina, only one of them will leave alive. Will Han Solo take the first shot?

SET HISTORY

Mos Eisley Cantina
Year 2004
Number 4501

Set name	Mos Eisley Cantina	
Year 2014	Number	75052
Pieces 615	Source	EP IV

Stolen stormtrooper armor

DL-44 blaster

Confident smirk

Scarf

Insulated jacket

Hood

FROZEN SMUGGLER
Two different versions of Han imprisoned in carbonite were produced for *Slave I* (set 8097) and Jabba's Palace (set 9516), more detailed than an earlier stickered tile version.

Utility belt

HAN SOLO (STORMTROOPER)

In the Death Star (set 10188, released in 2008), Solo, like Luke Skywalker, wears stolen stormtrooper armor to rescue Princess Leia.

HAN SOLO (ENDOR)

The A-wing starfighter (set 75003) includes Han as he appears at the Battle of Endor: with brown pants and his familiar black vest.

HAN SOLO (HOTH)

This 2013 Han minifigure in snow gear looks miserable—is it the chill of Hoth, the smell of tauntauns, or the perils of being wanted by bounty hunters?

Convenient handles

Space for minifigure to be slotted behind frozen Solo

HAN SOLO (CARBONITE)

▼ Millennium Falcon

After the disastrous Battle of Hoth, Han Solo and Chewbacca pilot the *Falcon* to Cloud City, with Princess Leia and C-3PO on board. Hinged exterior panels reveal the main hold (with chairs and hologame) and, at the rear, the hyperdrive and engine room. Minifigures can hide inside the concealed smuggling compartment, and two minifigures can aim and fire the ship's powerful quad laser cannons.

Set name	*Millennium Falcon*	
Year 2012		Number 7965
Pieces 1,238		Source EP IV & VI

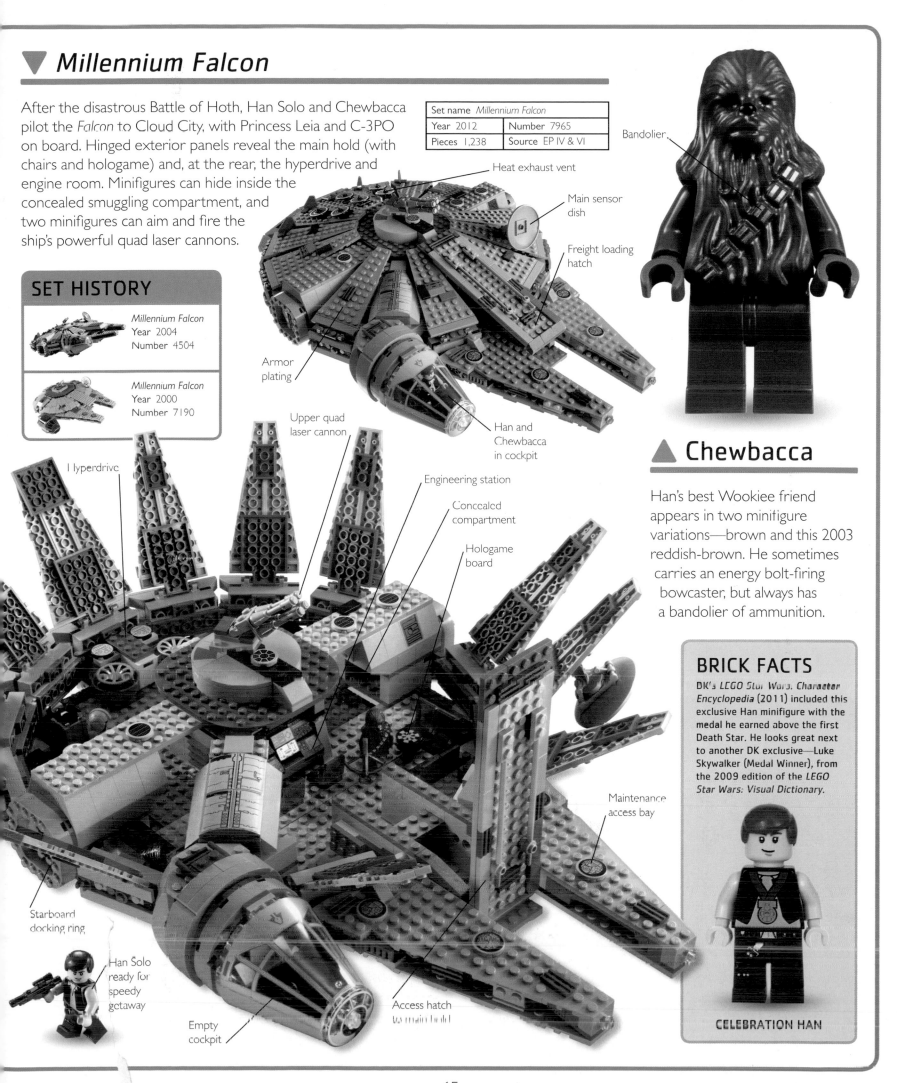

SET HISTORY

Millennium Falcon
Year 2004
Number 4504

Millennium Falcon
Year 2000
Number 7190

Heat exhaust vent

Main sensor dish

Freight loading hatch

Armor plating

Han and Chewbacca in cockpit

Hyperdrive

Upper quad laser cannon

Engineering station

Concealed compartment

Hologame board

Starboard docking ring

Han Solo ready for speedy getaway

Empty cockpit

Access hatch to main hold

Maintenance access bay

Bandolier

▲ Chewbacca

Han's best Wookiee friend appears in two minifigure variations—brown and this 2003 reddish-brown. He sometimes carries an energy bolt-firing bowcaster, but always has a bandolier of ammunition.

BRICK FACTS

DK's *LEGO Star Wars: Character Encyclopedia* (2011) included this exclusive Han minifigure with the medal he earned above the first Death Star. He looks great next to another DK exclusive—Luke Skywalker (Medal Winner), from the 2009 edition of the *LEGO Star Wars: Visual Dictionary*.

CELEBRATION HAN

Millennium Falcon

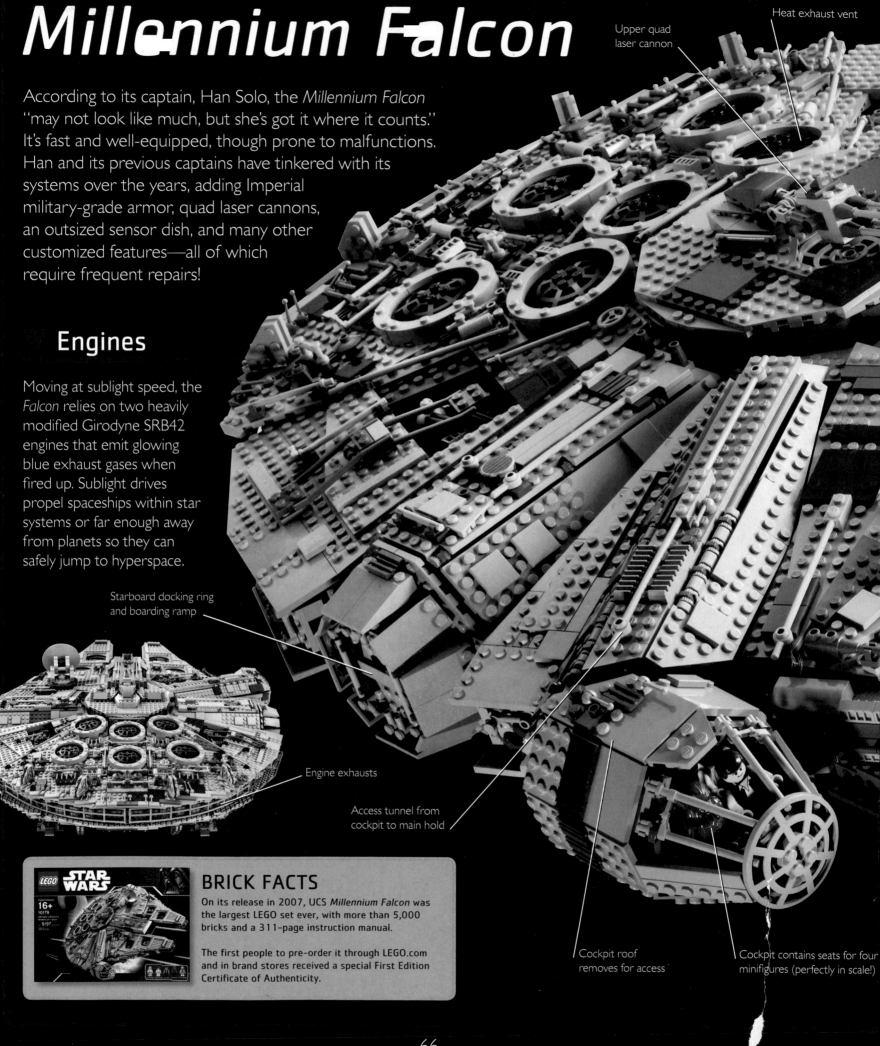

According to its captain, Han Solo, the *Millennium Falcon* "may not look like much, but she's got it where it counts." It's fast and well-equipped, though prone to malfunctions. Han and its previous captains have tinkered with its systems over the years, adding Imperial military-grade armor, quad laser cannons, an outsized sensor dish, and many other customized features—all of which require frequent repairs!

Engines

Moving at sublight speed, the *Falcon* relies on two heavily modified Girodyne SRB42 engines that emit glowing blue exhaust gases when fired up. Sublight drives propel spaceships within star systems or far enough away from planets so they can safely jump to hyperspace.

Upper quad laser cannon

Heat exhaust vent

Starboard docking ring and boarding ramp

Engine exhausts

Access tunnel from cockpit to main hold

Cockpit roof removes for access

Cockpit contains seats for four minifigures (perfectly in scale!)

BRICK FACTS

On its release in 2007, UCS *Millennium Falcon* was the largest LEGO set ever, with more than 5,000 bricks and a 311-page instruction manual.

The first people to pre-order it through LEGO.com and in brand stores received a special First Edition Certificate of Authenticity.

Main sensor dish elevates
and rotates

Quad Laser Cannons

A minifigure can sit in the gunner's seat facing upward
to operate the upper quad laser cannons, which rotate
for aiming and firing. The lower quad laser cannons
can also rotate on their turrets.

Luke in
gunner's seat

Maintenance
access bay

Armor plate

Freight loading
room

Front mandibles used in cargo transport
use extendible freight loading arms

Forward
floodlight

Boarding Ramp

The *Falcon*'s crew enter via a
retractable boarding ramp that
lowers from behind the starboard
docking ring. When in danger, Han
can't get inside there fast enough!

DATA FILE

Set name: *Millennium Falcon*
Year: 2007   **Set Number:** 10179
Pieces: 5,195   **Source:** IV, V, & VI
Dimensions:
length 84cm (33in)
width 56cm (22in)
height 21cm (8¼ in)
Minifigures: 5 (Han Solo, Chewbacca,
Luke Skywalker, Obi-Wan Kenobi, and
Princess Leia Organa)

Death Star

The Imperial battle station known as the Death Star is designed to quash potential dissent through displays of terrifying force. The first Death Star uses its superweapon to obliterate Princess Leia's home planet Alderaan. The second Death Star, though seemingly incomplete, is actually fully operational—and is intended to lure the rebels to their doom.

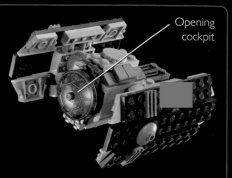

TIE ADVANCED
The mini-sized TIE Advanced is unique to the set. It can be flown into the hangar and docked on a slide-out TIE fighter rack. The cockpit viewscreen opens to allow Vader to take the controls.

Opening cockpit

Mechanism controls central turbolift

Rogue assassin droid

Protocol droid on work bench

Tool rack

Rotating turbolaser turret

TIE docking rack

TIE Advanced

Turbolaser turning mechanism

Grand Moff Tarkin

Emperor Palpatine's throne

Guard post

Elevator well

Collapsing catwalk

Vader duels with Luke

Railing

Air duct

Winch handle raises and lowers pilot lift

Stormtroopers on extendible bridge

Loading bay

Air shaft

Cargo crane

Cargo crate

R2-Q5

Luke and Leia prepare to swing across chasm

Storage bay

Central turbolift shaft

DATA FILE
Set name: Death Star
Year: 2008
Set Number: 10188
Pieces: 3,803
Source: EP IV & VI
Dimensions: length 42cm (16½ in); width 42cm (16½ in); height 41cm (16in)
Minifigures: 24—Luke Skywalker (in regular outfit, stormtrooper outfit, and Jedi Knight outfit), Han Solo (regular outfit and stormtrooper outfit), Obi-Wan Kenobi, C-3PO, R2-D2, Princess Leia, Chewbacca, Darth Vader, Grand Moff Tarkin, Emperor Palpatine, 2 stormtroopers, 2 Imperial guards, assassin droid, interrogation droid, Death Star droid, 2 Death Star troopers, R2-Q5, and mouse droid.

VIEWSCREEN DISPLAYS

A viewscreen in the superlaser control room displays tracking monitor readouts of Alderaan and the Fourth Moon of Yavin as it emerges from behind the planet itself into firing range.

▼ Two Death Stars in One

The Death Star set combines aspects of the first and second Death Stars. Luke, for example, appears three times: in stormtrooper uniform to rescue Leia, in his regular outfit to swing across the air shaft, and as a Jedi Knight to battle Darth Vader.

DETENTION CELL
In her detention cell, Princess Leia refuses to give Vader the location of the rebel base. She even stands firm against the interrogator droid's ultrasonic and electroshock devices. Finally Luke and Han arrive to rescue her—and they all dive into a filthy trash compactor!

Superlaser control room
Control mechanism for superlaser
Death Star trooper
Sensor array
Tributary laser beam
Turbolift entrance
Turbolift shaft
Turbolaser
Conference table (weapons cache underneath)
Security cameras
Cog opens cell door from prison block corridor
Interrogator droid
Removeable access panel to Leia's detention cell
Superlaser firing dish
Control station
Mechanism for closing trash compactor walls
Turbolaser cannon
Kenobi working in secret
Control lever
Tractor beam reactor coupling
C-3PO and R2-D2 keep a low profile

TURBOLASER CANNON
A Death Star trooper operates a rotating and firing turbolaser cannon against rebel X-wing starfighters.

Trash compactor wall

Doorway out of trash compactor

GARBAGE SQUID
Eye stem

Dianogas, or garbage squids, live in trash compactors, garbage pits, and sewers across the galaxy, feeding on scraps of decaying organic matter.

Tentacle

▲ Minifigures

The set features several unique minifigures, including Luke and Han in stormtrooper disguise, a white assassin droid, and Emperor Palpatine with a supremely grotesque face. Also, Darth Vader features a new torso design.

▶ Stormtrooper

Nameless, faceless stormtroopers are utterly loyal to the Empire. Minifigures appear either with or without mouth grilles (dotted mouths), and with black, yellow, or flesh-colored heads under their helmets.

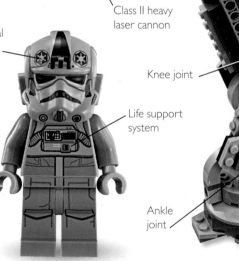

Polarizing filter lenses

E-11 blaster rifle

Heater controls

Imperial Army

At the end of the Clone Wars, the Galactic Republic becomes an Empire and its military resources now serve the new regime. Clone troopers become stormtroopers, their ranks made up of clones and, now, human recruits. Specialist stormtroopers are trained for a variety of military roles on land and in space.

▼ AT-AT Walker

Set name AT-AT Walker	
Year 2014	Number 75054
Pieces 1138	Source EP V & VI

SET HISTORY

 AT-AT
Year 2010
Number 8129

 Motorized Walking AT-AT
Year 2007
Number 10178

 AT-AT
Year 2003
Number 4483

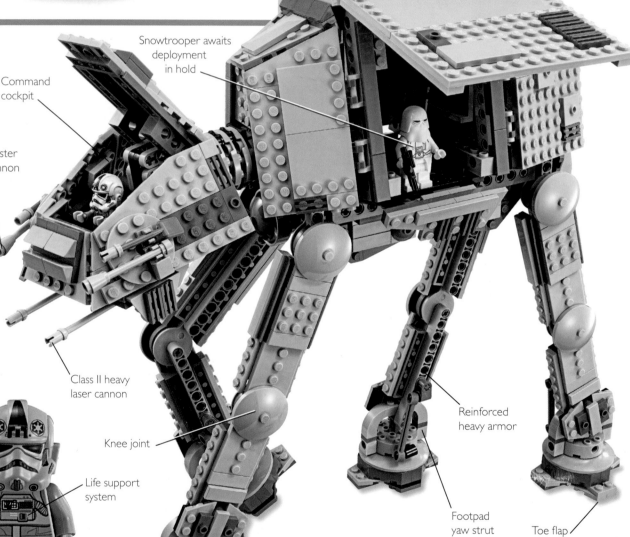

Snowtrooper awaits deployment in hold

Command cockpit

Blaster cannon

Class II heavy laser cannon

Knee joint

Life support system

Ankle joint

Reinforced heavy armor

Footpad yaw strut

Toe flap

Footpad

Macrobinoculars

Imperial symbol

GENERAL VEERS

General Veers masterminds the devastating assault on the rebel base on Hoth from the cockpit of the lead AT-AT.

AT-AT DRIVER

Equipped with insulated jumpsuits and life-support packs, AT-AT drivers guide the huge walkers.

During the Battle of Hoth, the Empire deploys All Terrain Armored Transports (AT-ATs) against the rebels, knowing the mere sight of these walking tanks is enough to terrify most soldiers. An AT-AT's side opens to reveal a staging platform for the two snowtrooper minifigures and General Veers, who stand ready to attack the rebel artillery. An AT-AT driver steers the walker from a cockpit in its head.

Battle of Hoth
Year 2013
Number 75014

Snowtrooper
Battle Pack
Year 2010
Number 8084

The Battle of Endor
Year 2009
Number 8038

AT-AT
Year 2003
Number 4483

Speeder Bike
Year 1999
Number 7128

▼ Speeder Bike

Whether on icy planets or moons thick with forests, Imperial troops rely on high-speed repulsorlift speeder bikes for antipersonnel or reconnaissance missions, supporting slower units such as AT-AT walkers.

Scout trooper

Turbine repulsorlift

Blaster pistol

Steering vanes

Brake pedal

Polarized visor

Set name	Ewok Village	
Year	2013	Number 10236
Pieces	1,990	Film EP VI

▶ E-Web Blaster

At the Battle of Hoth, snowtroopers use E-Web repeating blasters on tripods. These lightweight artillery pieces are carried by troops and can be rapidly assembled.

Set name	Battle of Hoth	
Year	2013	Number 75014
Pieces	426	Source EP IV & VI

▼ Sandtrooper

Electro pike

2014 sandtrooper

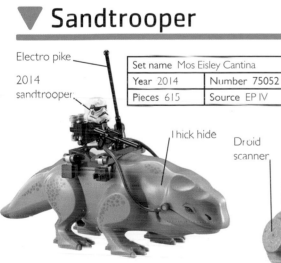

Thick hide

Droid scanner

On Tatooine, an Imperial sandtrooper with shoulder pauldron and backpack rebreather makes a search patrol on a dewback. Unlike some Imperial vehicles, these native lizards are not immobilized by sandstorms!

Snowtrooper in heated suit

Cannon barrel

Targeting grips

Flashback suppressor

AT-ST DRIVER

AT-ST drivers wear anti-shock helmets and jumpsuits.

▼ AT-ST

Imperial All Terrain Scout Transports (AT-ST) can run through rugged terrain on antipersonnel or reconnaissance missions. They are piloted from the cockpit in the head and are armed with blaster and concussion weapons.

Chewbacca after commandeering the AT-ST

Light blaster cannons

SET HISTORY

AT-ST
Year 2007
Number 7657

AT-ST
Year 2001
Number 7127

Set name	The Battle of Endor	
Year	2009	Number 8038
Pieces	890	Film EP VI

COLORFUL COMMAND

Sandtroopers' pauldrons indicate their rank, with orange for commanders and black for regular troops. A dirty sandtrooper with an orange pauldron comes with Droid Escape (set 9490), released in 2012.

Twin blaster cannons

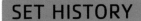

Imperial Navy

When Palpatine establishes his tyrannical Empire, the Republic's massive navy is appropriated and put to brutal use. Jedi-piloted Interceptor starfighters, with their solar-panel wings, are reborn as aggressive TIE fighters. Indeed, the Imperial fleet is expanded with a variety of new, ever-deadlier models, while Emperor Palpatine travels in an updated version of the shuttle he used as Supreme Chancellor.

Solar-panel wing

Main viewport

Cockpit hatch

Laser tip

Energy collection array

Support frame

▶ TIE Fighter

TIE fighters are armed with cannons and have no deflector shields or hyperdrive, making them light and agile in battle. Set 7146 (2001) comes with a pilot, stormtrooper, and service rack (which doubles as a display stand). Set 7263 (2005) stands by itself on its wings. It includes a pilot and Darth Vader with a light-up saber. Set 9492 (2012) has a gray (rather than blue) color palette and new borders on the wings. A pilot, a Death Star Trooper, an astromech, and an Imperial officer are included.

SET HISTORY

TIE Fighter
Year 2005
Number 7263

TIE Fighter/
TIE Collection
Year 2001/2003
Number 7146/10131

Set name	TIE Fighter	
Year	2012	Number 9492
Pieces	413	Source EP IV & VI

Helmet hides smiling face

Spacesuit

Acoustic signaler

TIE FIGHTER PILOT
Imperial fighter pilots are a specially trained, elite flying corps.

R5-J2
An Imperial astromech, R5-J2 boasts a redesigned, movie-accurate head mold.

▼ Landing Craft

Like *Lambda*-class shuttles, *Sentinel*-class landing craft have a fixed central wing and two side wings that fold up when landing. They carry detachments of stormtroopers throughout the galaxy (the set comes with two stormtroopers and two sandtroopers). Piloted by an Imperial pilot, the ship boasts laser cannons, firing rockets, and four concussion missiles (released by pressing bricks in the rear).

Hinged cockpit

Laser cannon

Gear system operates wings

Set name	Imperial Landing Craft	
Year	2007	Number 7659
Pieces	471	Source EP IV

▼ Turbolaser

Turbolasers are heavy laser-cannon emplacements housed on large warships or space stations. When rebel X-wings and Y-wings attack the first Death Star, black-suited gun crews rush to thousands of turbolasers, blasting away at the swarming fighters.

Flick-fire missile

Set name	Death Star Troopers	
Year	2014	Number 75034
Pieces	100	Source EP IV

Set name	TIE Fighter Collection
Year 2004	Number 10131
Pieces 682	Source EU

High-performance solar panels

Droid brain pod

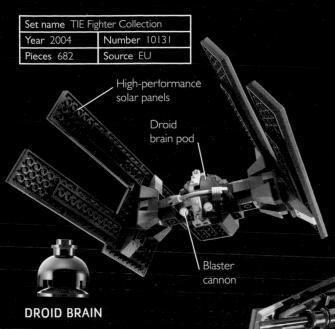

Blaster cannon

DROID BRAIN

▲ TIE-D

Shortly after the Battle of Endor, the Empire developed prototype pilotless fighters with programmable droid brains. The droid brain minifigure can be removed from the pod casing.

▼ TIE Interceptor

The TIE Interceptor is the fastest, most maneuverable, and best-armed starfighter in the Imperial fleet. Its upgraded ion engines deliver immense power for dogfights, and each wing-tip boasts a deadly blaster cannon whose linked fire can rip through enemy fighters.

Set name TIE Interceptor	
Year 2006	Number 6206
Pieces 212	Source EP VI

Wing-tip blaster cannon

Angled solar wing

Cut-away wing profile

Advanced targeting sensors

TIE minifigure pilot in cockpit

◄ TIE Bomber

Single-pilot TIE bombers make precise "surgical strikes" that would be impractical for the Empire's capital ships. The ship's armaments include laser weapons and proton bombs that can be deployed against shielded targets, blasting open their hiding places.

Solar-panel wings

Cockpit viewscreen

AWAITING MUNITIONS

Spring-loaded guided concussion missile port

Set name TIE Bomber	
Year 2003	Number 4479
Pieces 229	Source EP V

Blaster rack

Shadowtrooper in cockpit

Stormtrooper awaiting deployment

Set name Imperial Dropship	
Year 2008	Number 7667
Pieces 81	Source EU

▲ Dropship

Dropships are lightly armed troop transports. A shadowtrooper sits in the cockpit and the detachable troop platform seats four stormtroopers (the set has three).

Star Destroyer

Dagger-shaped Star Destroyers are the most feared symbol of Imperial might, armed with deadly firepower and powerful scanner and tractor-beam arrays. The Republic develops *Victory*-class Star Destroyers as capital ships in the final years of the Clone Wars, and the Emperor expands the fleet with new *Imperial*-class Star Destroyers, employed to crush and subdue worlds.

▼ Meditation Chamber

On long space voyages, Darth Vader sits in his meditation chamber, or hyperbaric pod. In the high-pressure air mix within the chamber, Vader can remove his helmet (using a lifting mechanism) to reveal his horribly scarred face and head.

▼ Escape Pod

The ship contains a life-support escape pod for emergency evacuations. Escape pods contain food and oxygen, as well as flares, a porta-shelter, and survival suits for passengers.

Distress beacon

Rocket thruster

Repulsor soft-landing coils

Fuel cell

▶ Forward Systems

A Star Destroyer's nose contains powerful pursuit tractor beams. The model contains a mechanism that, when pulled, ejects the escape pod through a hatch in the ship's underside.

COMMAND BRIDGE
The bridge is situated at the center of the command tower, in view of any ship under attack. Grand Moff Tarkin and an Imperial officer stand at the flight consoles and tracking systems.

Defense turret

Armored hull

MSE-6 droid

R2-D5

Grand Moff Tarkin

Flight deck

Escape pod

Escape pod release mechanism

Entrance to escape pod hangar bay

SET HISTORY

Star destroyer
Year 2014
Number 75055

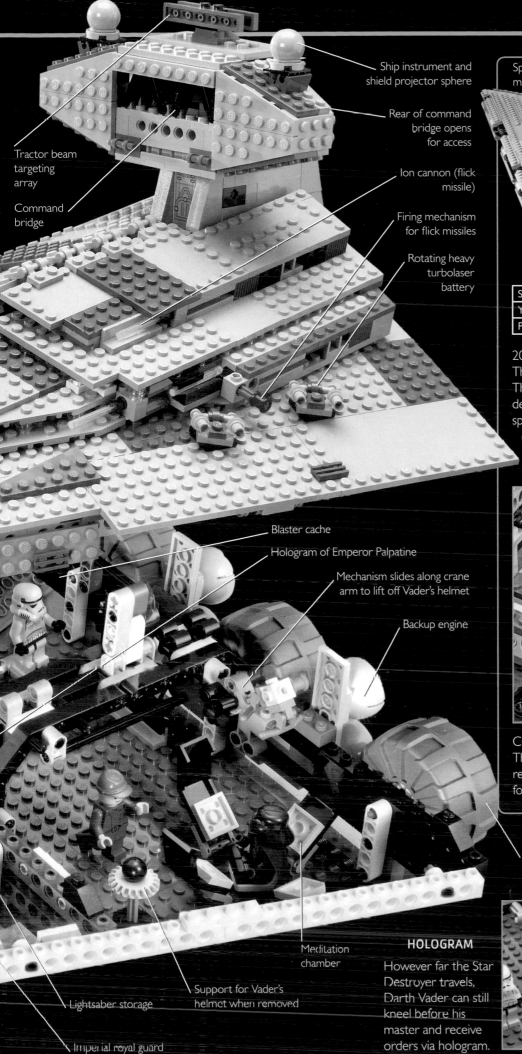

Ship instrument and shield projector sphere

Tractor beam targeting array

Command bridge

Rear of command bridge opens for access

Ion cannon (flick missile)

Firing mechanism for flick missiles

Rotating heavy turbolaser battery

Blaster cache

Hologram of Emperor Palpatine

Mechanism slides along crane arm to lift off Vader's helmet

Backup engine

Support for Vader's helmet when removed

Lightsaber storage

Imperial royal guard

Meditation chamber

Main engine thrust nozzle

HOLOGRAM
However far the Star Destroyer travels, Darth Vader can still kneel before his master and receive orders via hologram.

Spring-loaded missile launcher

Wheel hub caps used for engine clusters

Set name	Star Destroyer	
Year 2014		Number 75055
Pieces 1175		Source IV, V, VI

2014 STAR DESTROYER
The imposing warship was redesigned and updated in 2014. The interior features a movie-accurate bridge with stickers depicting the controls and its exterior features brand-new spring-loaded bricks that can fire missiles at approaching enemy vehicles.

Hologram projector

Death Star telemetry screen

COMM STATION
The communication station is where Imperial officers receive orders from the Empire and occasionally from the foreboding Emperor himself!

DATA FILE
Set name: Imperial Star Destroyer
Year: 2006 **Set Number:** 6211
Pieces: 1,367 **Source:** IV, V, & VI
Dimensions:
length 74.4cm (29 in)
width 38.4cm (15 in)
height 9.3cm (3.7 in)
Minifigures: 9 (Darth Vader, Grand Moff Tarkin, Imperial officer, two stormtroopers, two Imperial guards, R2-Q5, MSE-6 droid)

Cloud City

After the Battle of Hoth, Han Solo and Chewbacca escape with Leia and C-3PO to a floating pleasure resort and mining colony called Cloud City, located near a gas planet called Bespin. Its administrator, Lando Calrissian, is Han Solo's longtime friend and sometime rival. The arrival of Solo and the others, however, is preceded by Boba Fett and Darth Vader, who spring a trap and lure Luke Skywalker to a confrontation with Vader himself!

LEIA ORGANA
In the luxurious surroundings of Cloud City, Leia changes clothes, lets down her hair, and ties it back. Succumbing to Solo's charms, she has only a brief time to relax before she is ensnared in Vader's trap.

LEIA (BESPIN)

▼ Duel with Vader

When Luke arrives at Cloud City to rescue his friends, Vader is waiting for him in the carbon freezing chamber. They ignite their lightsabers and duel through the chamber into a control room overlooking a huge reactor shaft. Luke is sucked through a smashed window and a final clash takes place on a treacherous gantry.

Viewport

Pipes in control room

Mechanism allows wall to drop

Doorway to landing platform

Sculpture

Balcony over reactor shaft

Mechanism to open viewport

Dining room table

COLLAPSING WALLS
Darth Vader uses the Force to throw objects at Luke. Watch out for that collapsing wall, Luke!

THROUGH THE WINDOW
A viewport breaks open and a vacuum sucks Luke onto a narrow maintenance gantry, where the final confrontation occurs.

▼ Landing Platform

Arriving starships usually dock on a landing platform outside the main wall of Cloud City. When Han and the others arrive in the *Millennium Falcon*, Lando Calrissian meets them. Later, he escorts Han and his friends to a dining room—but it's a trap. The Dark Lord of the Sith and his stormtroopers are waiting to capture them.

BESPIN GUARD
Sergeant Edian is a loyal member of the Bespin security forces, called the Wing Guard. He helps escort the carbon-frozen Han Solo onto Boba Fett's *Slave I* and his minifigure appears in *Slave I* (set 6209).

SERGEANT EDIAN

Landing lights

Entrance walkway

Carbon Freezing Chamber

HAN SOLO IN CARBONITE

Vader intends to carbon freeze Luke for transport to the Emperor, and decides to test the process on Han Solo. Watched by Calrissian, Vader, and Fett, Solo is lowered into the freezing chamber: he emerges frozen into a block of carbonite.

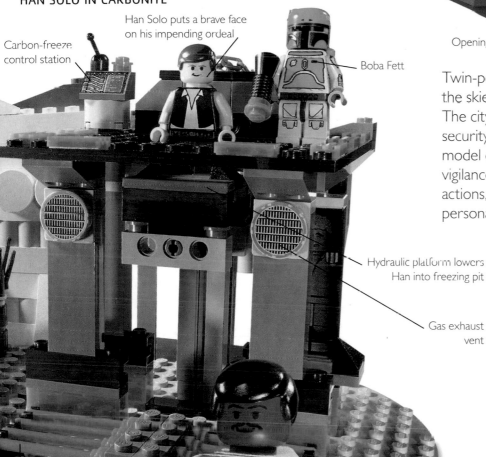

Han Solo puts a brave face on his impending ordeal

Carbon-freeze control station

Boba Fett

Hydraulic platform lowers Han into freezing pit

Gas exhaust vent

Atmospheric elements

Custom-made shirt

Dashing cape

LANDO CALRISSIAN

Lando Calrissian is an ex-card shark who used his winning charms and sartorial style to become the baron-administrator of Cloud City. At first, Vader forces him to betray Solo, but Lando turns against the Imperials and eventually becomes a general in the Rebel Alliance.

Cloud Car

Passenger cabin

Lobot in pilot cockpit

Opening maintenance hatch

Opening side hatch

Twin-pod cloud cars patrol the skies of Cloud City. The city's Wing Guard security forces use an armed model of the cloud car for vigilance and emergency actions, though Lobot's personal cloud car is unarmed.

Set name	Twin-Pod Cloud Car	
Year 2002	Number 7119	
Pieces 117	Source EP V	

LOYAL AIDE
Lobot is Lando Calrissian's aide and Cloud City's computer liaison officer. He has a brain-enhancing device wrapped around the back of his skull that enables him to interface directly with the city's central computer.

LOBOT

DATA FILE
Set name: Cloud City
Year: 2003
Set Number: 10123
Pieces: 705
Source: EP V
Dimensions:
length 57.5cm (22⅝ in);
width 7cm (2¾ in);
height 38cm (15in)
Minifigures: 7 (Luke Skywalker, Han Solo, Leia Organa, Lando Calrissian, Darth Vader, Boba Fett, stormtrooper)

BRICK FACTS
Boba Fett's minifigure has appeared exclusively in gold, silver, bronze, and white, but this Cloud City variation from 2003 is the only one to have rare printing on the arms.

BOBA FETT

Rebel Alliance

Freedom fighters who have banded together as the Rebel Alliance are dedicated to the Empire's downfall. Some rebels are deserters from the Imperial forces, but many are untrained volunteers. With skillful leaders and a ragtag assortment of ships and weapons, the rebels prove a serious threat to Emperor Palpatine's iron rule.

▼ Y-Wing Fighter

BTL-A4 Y-wings are old but tough workhorses of the rebel fleet, famously employed in the attacks on both Death Stars. They have hyperdrives, ion fission engines, and massive firepower, including ion cannons and laser weapons. Gold Leader's Y-wing swoops into battle armed with a swiveling gun turret, torpedos, and flick-fire missiles.

SET HISTORY

Anakin's Y-Wing Starfighter
Year 2009
Number 8037

Y-Wing Fighter
Year 2007
Number 7658

TIE Fighter & Y-Wing
Year 2002
Number 7152

Laser-tip cannons

Swiveling ion cannons

Gold Leader in cockpit

Astromech droid socket

Sensor dome

Thrust vectral ring

Bomb bay loading hatch

Ion jet enginet

Set name	Gold Leader's Y-Wing Starfighter	
Year 2012	Number	9495
Pieces 458	Source	EP IV & VI

ENGINEER CORPS
Rebel engineers and technicians maintain and repair spaceships and vehicles, among other tasks.

REBEL TECHNICIAN

R5-F7 (2012)
An astromech assigned to Yavin 4's Massassi Base, R5-F7 is blown apart in the fierce fight above the first Death Star.

DUTCH VANDER (2012)
A veteran pilot, Dutch flies as Gold Leader at the Battle of Yavin. His orange visor and chin strap are printed details on his head.

High-visibility flight suit for rescue operations

▼ Rebel Scout Speeder

The rebels use these military-grade repulsorlift speeders for patrol and reconnaissance. They seat a pilot, gunner, and two soldiers. The rotating heavy laser cannon detaches for use as a static emplacement.

Set name	Rebel Scout Speeder	
Year 2008	Number	7668
Pieces 82	Source	EU

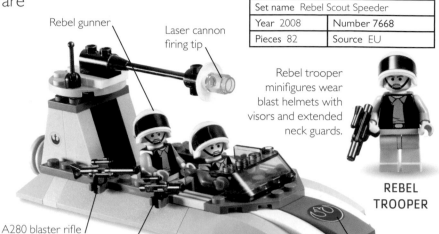

Rebel gunner

Laser cannon firing tip

A280 blaster rifle

DH-17 blaster

Rebel insignia

Rebel trooper minifigures wear blast helmets with visors and extended neck guards.

REBEL TROOPER

◄ Wedge Antilles

A capable pilot, Wedge is one of the few survivors of the battle above the first Death Star. He destroys an AT-AT walker on Hoth and fights bravely under the callsign Red Leader at the climactic Battle of Endor. His minifigure is included with X-Wing Fighter (set 6212), released in 2006.

▼ Tantive IV

As a senator for Alderaan, Princess Leia Organa travels in a diplomatic starship, the *Tantive IV*. The ship also carries out covert missions for the Rebel Alliance—until Darth Vader pursues the ship and captures it.

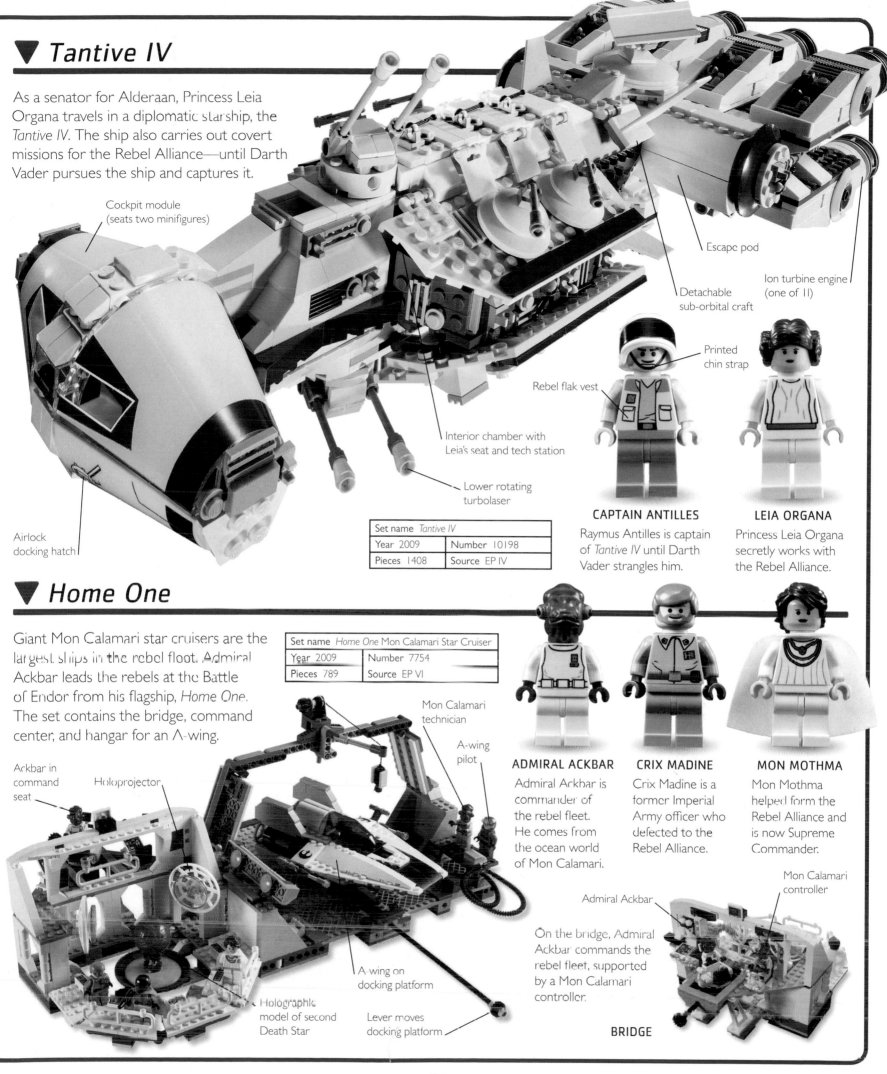

Cockpit module (seats two minifigures)

Escape pod

Ion turbine engine (one of 11)

Detachable sub-orbital craft

Printed chin strap

Rebel flak vest

Interior chamber with Leia's seat and tech station

Lower rotating turbolaser

Airlock docking hatch

Set name	*Tantive IV*	
Year	2009	Number	10198
Pieces	1408	Source	EP IV

CAPTAIN ANTILLES

Raymus Antilles is captain of *Tantive IV* until Darth Vader strangles him.

LEIA ORGANA

Princess Leia Organa secretly works with the Rebel Alliance.

▼ Home One

Giant Mon Calamari star cruisers are the largest ships in the rebel fleet. Admiral Ackbar leads the rebels at the Battle of Endor from his flagship, *Home One*. The set contains the bridge, command center, and hangar for an A-wing.

Set name	*Home One* Mon Calamari Star Cruiser	
Year	2009	Number	7754
Pieces	789	Source	EP VI

Mon Calamari technician

A-wing pilot

Ackbar in command seat

Holoprojector

A-wing on docking platform

Holographic model of second Death Star

Lever moves docking platform

ADMIRAL ACKBAR

Admiral Ackbar is commander of the rebel fleet. He comes from the ocean world of Mon Calamari.

CRIX MADINE

Crix Madine is a former Imperial Army officer who defected to the Rebel Alliance.

MON MOTHMA

Mon Mothma helped form the Rebel Alliance and is now Supreme Commander.

Admiral Ackbar

Mon Calamari controller

On the bridge, Admiral Ackbar commands the rebel fleet, supported by a Mon Calamari controller.

BRIDGE

Echo Base

On the ice planet Hoth, the Rebel Alliance establishes its secret Echo Base, protected by an immense energy shield. When the Empire discovers the location of the base, it deploys AT-ATs and AT-STs to destroy the shield generator. The combined strength of rebel artillery emplacements and snowspeeder squadrons cannot prevent one of the worst battlefield defeats for the Alliance.

PROTOCOL DROIDS
K-3PO is a white protocol droid who was given the rank of lieutenant in Hoth Rebel Base (set 7666). Exclusive to Hoth Echo Base (set 7879), R-3PO has special programming designed to ferret out Imperial spies.

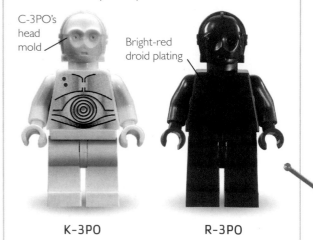

C-3PO's head mold

Bright-red droid plating

K-3PO

R-3PO

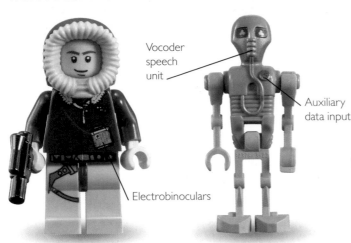

Vocoder speech unit

Auxiliary data input

Breath mask

Harness

Electrobinoculars

Weights anchor body

HAN ON HOTH

Han's blue parka hood with tan fur trim can be swapped for the Corellian's usual mop of brown hair.

2-1B MEDICAL DROID

2-1B's head and torso are a single, highly detailed piece, and his hand grips are set at right angles to each other.

BACTA-TANK LUKE

Clad in space skivvies for a healing dip in the bacta tank, this Luke minifigure has two faces: swivel his head to reveal a weary Luke with a tentative smile.

Rotating gun turrets with flick missiles

Slide out pin to activate icicle trap

Icicle

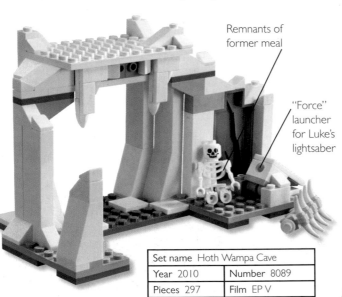

Remnants of former meal

"Force" launcher for Luke's lightsaber

P-Tower laser cannon

Set name	Hoth Wampa Cave	
Year	2010	Number 8089
Pieces	297	Film EP V

▲ **Wampa Cave**

After a Wampa captures Luke, the rebel hero must use the Force to escape the beast. Minifigures can attach to the Wampa's hand, but the ice monster also has an oversized turkey leg in case his prey should elude him.

WAMPA

Warning placard

Portable power unit

Catch secures base in "closed" play mode

Hoth Base (2007)

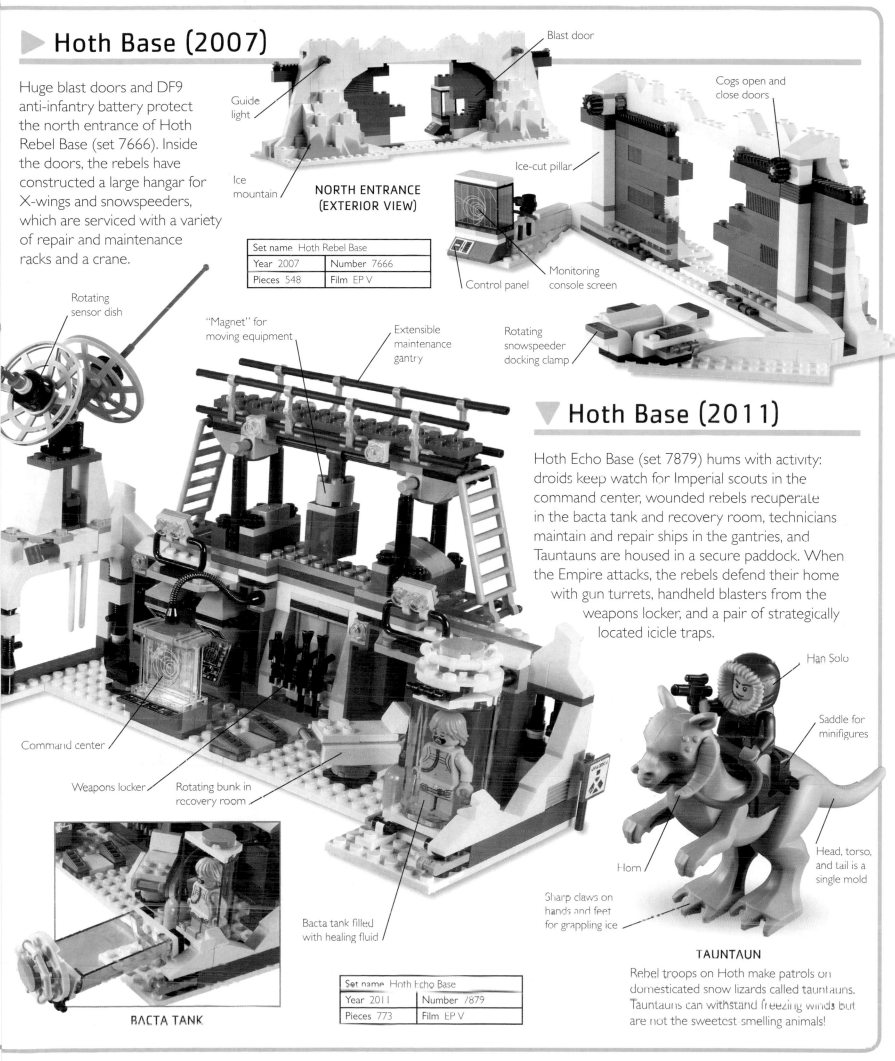

Huge blast doors and DF9 anti-infantry battery protect the north entrance of Hoth Rebel Base (set 7666). Inside the doors, the rebels have constructed a large hangar for X-wings and snowspeeders, which are serviced with a variety of repair and maintenance racks and a crane.

Guide light

Blast door

Cogs open and close doors

Ice-cut pillar

Ice mountain

NORTH ENTRANCE (EXTERIOR VIEW)

Set name	Hoth Rebel Base	
Year 2007	Number 7666	
Pieces 548	Film EP V	

Control panel

Monitoring console screen

Rotating sensor dish

"Magnet" for moving equipment

Extensible maintenance gantry

Rotating snowspeeder docking clamp

Hoth Base (2011)

Hoth Echo Base (set 7879) hums with activity: droids keep watch for Imperial scouts in the command center, wounded rebels recuperate in the bacta tank and recovery room, technicians maintain and repair ships in the gantries, and Tauntauns are housed in a secure paddock. When the Empire attacks, the rebels defend their home with gun turrets, handheld blasters from the weapons locker, and a pair of strategically located icicle traps.

Command center

Weapons locker

Rotating bunk in recovery room

Bacta tank filled with healing fluid

Han Solo

Saddle for minifigures

Head, torso, and tail is a single mold

Horn

Sharp claws on hands and feet for grappling ice

BACTA TANK

Set name	Hoth Echo Base	
Year 2011	Number 7879	
Pieces 773	Film EP V	

TAUNTAUN

Rebel troops on Hoth make patrols on domesticated snow lizards called tauntauns. Tauntauns can withstand freezing winds but are not the sweetest-smelling animals!

Jabba the Hutt

A gigantic, slug-like Hutt with slimy skin, an unfathomable appetite, and a large, lascivious mouth, Jabba lives to strike shady deals with other members of the galactic underworld. He is protected by thugs and hirelings on whose loyalty he keeps a careful eye. Luke Skywalker and his friends seek to rescue Han Solo from Jabba's clutches, but run the risk of falling prey to the gangster's wiles and becoming his latest victims.

Many chins

Belly swollen with gorg snacks

Muscular tail

JABBA THE HUTT (2012)

▼ Crime Lord

The first LEGO form of Jabba the Hutt from 2003 was a three-piece mold with no decoration. In 2012, the LEGO Group created an all-new Hutt in a single mold, with printed details. His decoration includes a tan face, extra wrinkles of flesh, catlike eyes, and even a tattoo on his meaty arm. This more fearsome Jabba appears in Jabba's Palace (set 9516) and Jabba's Sail Barge (set 75020).

Shrewd expression

◀ Main Entrance

C-3PO and R2-D2 tremble at the entry portcullis to Jabba's Palace (at least, C-3PO does!). A gatewatcher droid pokes its single photoreceptor through a slot in the door and passes news of their arrival to Jabba's henchman, Bib Fortuna, who interrogates them. After 2012, this scene was re-created within Jabba's Palace (set 9516).

Gates shared with several LEGO sets

Door slides open

Gatewatcher droid

R2-D2

C-3PO

Piercing red eyes

Lekku (headtails)

Breastplate

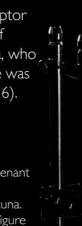

BIB FORTUNA

Jabba's chief lieutenant is a male Twi'lek named Bib Fortuna. His first minifigure appeared in Jabba's Message (set 4475).

BRICK FACTS
Jabba's Message (set 4475) and Jabba's Prize (set 4476) can clip onto the sides of Jabba's Palace (set 4480).

Set name	Jabba's Message	
Year	2003	Number 4475
Pieces	44	Source EP IV, V, & VI

Trophy Wall

Jabba tauntingly displays his prized trophy: Han Solo flash-frozen in carbonite. This simplified version of Han is found in earlier sets released until 2003.

Set name	Jabba's Prize	
Year	2003	Number 4476
Pieces	39	Source EP IV, V, & VI

Jabba's favorite decoration

Boba Fett stands guard

Rotta

Jabba's son, Rotta the Huttlet, can be clipped onto a minifigure's hand through a circle at his base. He comes with AT-TE Walker (set 7675) and The *Twilight* (set 7680), which re-creates his kidnap and rescue at the beginning of *Star Wars: The Clone Wars*.

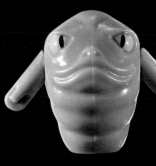

Vibro-ax

HENCHMEN The first LEGO version of the Gamorrean Guard, released in Jabba's Prize (set 4476) in 2003 is a simple, unique "sandwich board" over a torso and gray arms. This 2006 variant has brown arms. The 2012 version is more detailed (see p89).

GAMORREAN GUARD

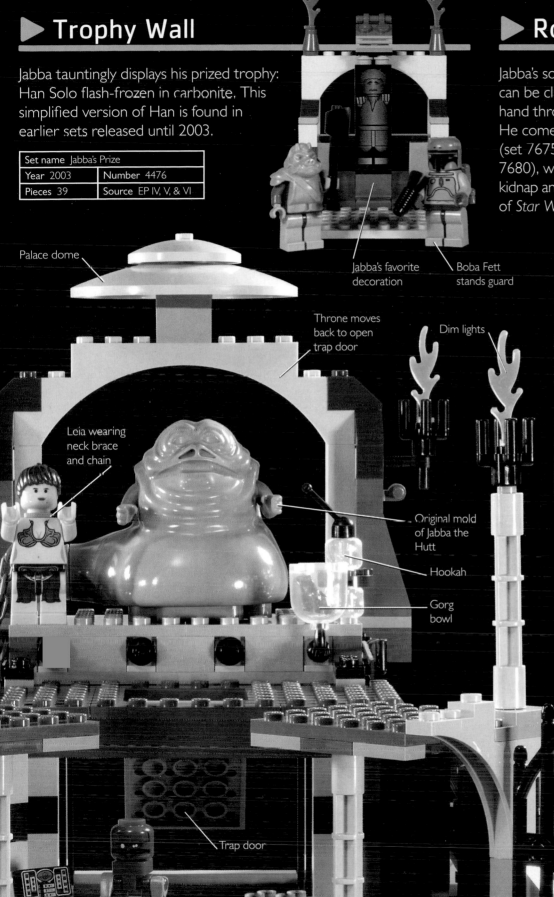

Palace dome

Throne moves back to open trap door

Dim lights

Leia wearing neck brace and chain

Original mold of Jabba the Hutt

Hookah

Gorg bowl

Trap door

EV-9D9

GNK droid

Droid "assessment" room

Throne Room

Jabba the Hutt sits atop a dais in his dimly lit throne room, within reach of a bowl of his favorite snack, slimy gorgs. He controls everything in the room, including a trap door that leads to a pit below. Enslaved Princess Leia has no choice but to watch as Jabba deals harshly with Luke Skywalker, now wearing the robes of a Jedi Knight. Beneath the throne room, droid supervisor EV-9D9 shows no mercy to a lost GNK droid.

SET HISTORY

Jabba's Palace
Year 2012
Number 9516

Set name	Jabba's Palace	
Year	2003	Number 4480
Pieces	234	Source EP IV, V, & VI

Jabba's Palace

In 2012, LEGO designers retraveled the lonely road that crosses the Dune Sea leading to the forbidding fortress of Jabba the Hutt. The revised palace is overrun with gangsters, bounty hunters, exotic creatures, cruel droids, entertainers, and servants. Rather than just re-creating the palace itself, the designers also produced a second set designed to stack underneath the throne room set—the dingy dungeon where the deadly rancor lives.

▶ Throne Room

Jabba's palace once belonged to the mysterious order of B'omarr monks who continue to go about their business on the lower levels. The palace is armed against external attacks with gun emplacements and missiles, and further dangers await those foolish enough to enter. The fortress is riddled with secret compartments, trap doors, and other unwelcome surprises—not to mention the depraved thugs and criminals who call its dank passages home.

Helmet

Thermal detonator

Electrostaff

BOUSHH
To infiltrate Jabba's lair on Tatooine, Princess Leia disguises herself as Boushh—a Ubese bounty hunter who has captured Chewbacca. When Jabba balks at the price for the Wookiee, Boushh threatens to blow up his palace with a thermal detonator—a gutsy move that earns Jabba's respect.

SET HISTORY

Jabba's Palace
Year 2003
Number 4480

Set name	Jabba's Palace		
Year	2012	Number	9516
Pieces	717	Source	EP VI

▶ Trap Door

Rebuffing Jabba's affections is a fatal mistake for the Twi'lek dancer Oola: Jabba mashes down on a hidden switch and drops her into the rancor pit. Here, sliding a lever seals poor Oola's fate.

Lookout post

Gamorrean guard

Trap door

Guard tower

Weapons cache

Binoculars

Boushh

Hookah

Salacious B. Crumb

Flick-fire missile defends palace

Domed temple roof

Jabba the Hutt seated on dais

Chewbacca

Han Solo frozen in carbonite

Lever opens trap door to rancor pit

Entrance door

B'omarr monk

▲ Guarded Entrance

C-3PO and R2-D2 discover that Jabba doesn't give visitors a warm welcome: a sentry droid interrogates those who arrive at the palace entrance, with swiveling guns ready to fire from above.

Sentry droid

Locked exit gate

Unfortunate Gamorrean guard

▶ Jabba's Minions

SALACIOUS B. CRUMB

This Kowakian monkey-lizard, made from a single LEGO piece, serves as court jester. He loves to cackle at guests' misfortunes.

GAMORREAN GUARD

These piglike guards serve Jabba as dim-witted muscle. This third incarnation has printed legs and a torso rich in detail.

B'OMARR MONK

These strange monks house their brains in jars ferried around by spiderlike droid bodies. The monks' legs are repurposed samurai swords.

MALAKILI

A tubby human, Malakili cares for Jabba's fearsome rancor. Swiveling his head reveals a tearful alternate face—Malakili is fond of the beast.

OOLA

A green-skinned Twi'lek female with printed details and a unique head piece, Oola falls through the trap door and is eaten by the hungry rancor.

BIB FORTUNA

The Twi'lek Bib Fortuna is Jabba's chief lieutenant. An earlier version of Bib with a milder expression appeared in Jabba's Message (set 4475).

RANCOR

Moveable arms and jointed fingers

Rancor is 10cm (3 in) tall

Remains of the rancor's earlier victim

Walls hewn from Tatooine rock

Luke Skywalker

Rancor

▲ Rancor Pit

Set name	Rancor Pit		
Year	2013	Number	75005
Pieces	380	Source	EP VI

The first LEGO rancor dwells beneath Jabba's throne room, devouring those who anger the cruel Hutt. The set stacks with Jabba's Palace, with a trap door so a minifigure can fall between sets, while Jabba's minions watch from above through the grate. A portcullis keeps the rancor in its dreary pen. Accessories include a key, pitchfork, and bucket.

Jabba's Sail Barge

Jabba's Sail Barge is a giant repulsorlift pleasure craft that carries the crime lord and his undesirable entourage from his palace to Podraces, gladiatorial contests, and other shadier activities. It also transports Jabba to the Great Pit of Carkoon to watch Luke Skywalker being fed to the hungry beast that inhabits this basin in the desert.

Decorative sails for shade, rather than propulsion

Observation deck

Fabric sails

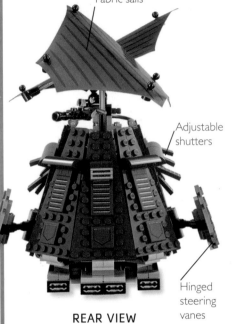

Adjustable shutters

Hinged steering vanes

REAR VIEW

▶ The *Khetanna*

No respectable—or unrespectable—Hutt is complete without an opulent sail barge. Originally just a traveling pleasure craft, the *Khetanna* has been upgraded with prison cells, guards, armor plating, and a custom-mounted deck gun—testament to Jabba's need for protection from rival gangs. Jabba's 2013 LEGO sail barge also has the addition of a large cannon that slides out of the heavily armored hull. Three sides of the model fold down so that Jabba has a ringside view of Luke's planned execution, without the inconvenience of leaving his throne room.

Cannon slides out

Decorative hull plating

Craft "floats" on hidden wheels

Exploratory tentacle

▼ Sand Skiff

Sand skiffs are repulsorlift platforms used to ferry passengers or prisoners to and from Jabba's palace. Luke is forced to walk the extensible plank over the Sarlacc pit.

Kithaba the bounty hunter

Lando disguised as skiff guard

Beaked tongue

Teeth prevent victims escaping

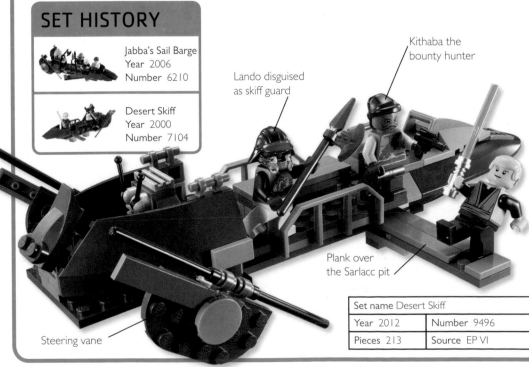

Plank over the Sarlacc pit

Steering vane

Set name Desert Skiff	
Year 2012	Number 9496
Pieces 213	Source EP VI

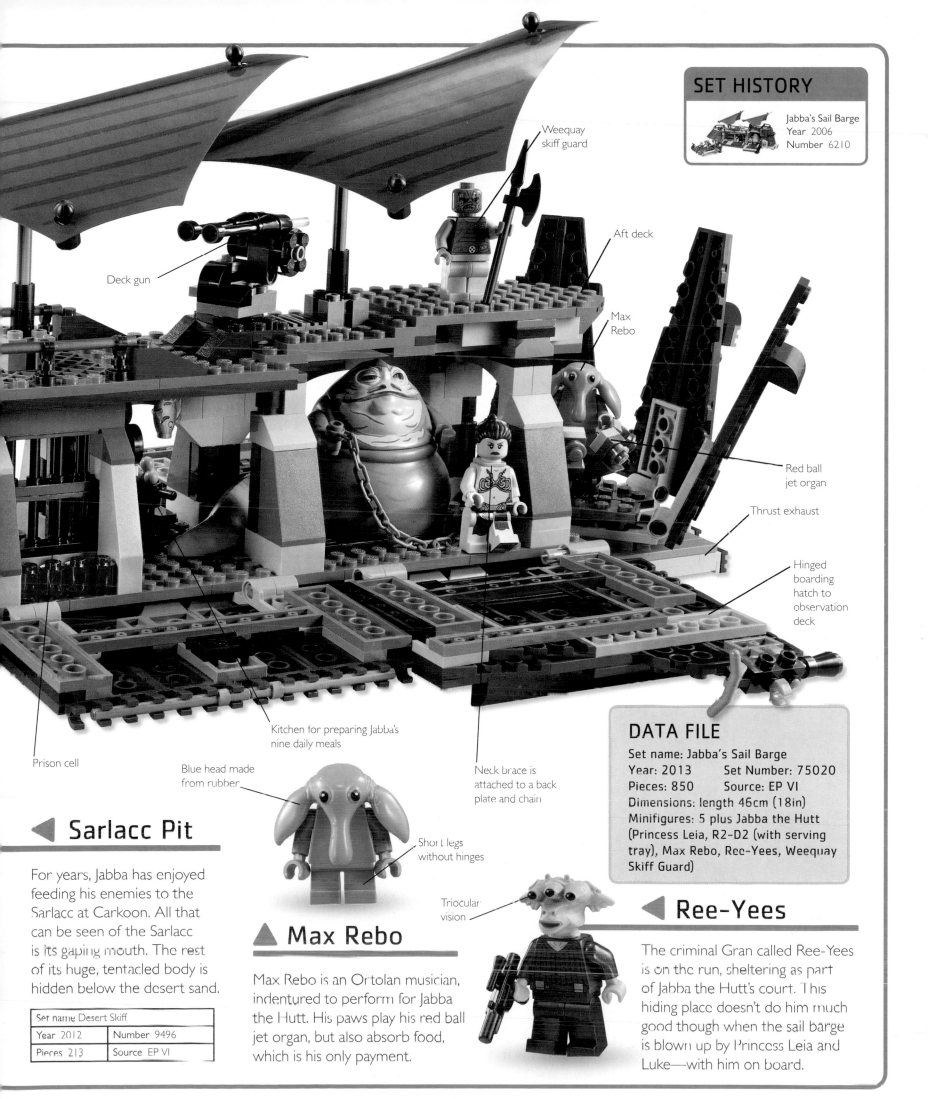

Weequay
skiff guard

Deck gun

Aft deck

Max
Rebo

Red ball
jet organ

Thrust exhaust

Hinged
boarding
hatch to
observation
deck

Kitchen for preparing Jabba's
nine daily meals

Neck brace is
attached to a back
plate and chain

Prison cell

Blue head made
from rubber

Short legs
without hinges

◀ Sarlacc Pit

For years, Jabba has enjoyed
feeding his enemies to the
Sarlacc at Carkoon. All that
can be seen of the Sarlacc
is its gaping mouth. The rest
of its huge, tentacled body is
hidden below the desert sand.

Set name Desert Skiff	
Year 2012	Number 9496
Pieces 213	Source EP VI

▲ Max Rebo

Max Rebo is an Ortolan musician,
indentured to perform for Jabba
the Hutt. His paws play his red ball
jet organ, but also absorb food,
which is his only payment.

Triocular
vision

DATA FILE

Set name: Jabba's Sail Barge
Year: 2013   Set Number: 75020
Pieces: 850   Source: EP VI
Dimensions: length 46cm (18in)
Minifigures: 5 plus Jabba the Hutt
(Princess Leia, R2-D2 (with serving
tray), Max Rebo, Ree-Yees, Weequay
Skiff Guard)

◀ Ree-Yees

The criminal Gran called Ree-Yees
is on the run, sheltering as part
of Jabba the Hutt's court. This
hiding place doesn't do him much
good though when the sail barge
is blown up by Princess Leia and
Luke—with him on board.

▼ A-Wing Fighter

The rebels constructed this small, lightning-fast ship in secret before the Battle of Endor as an escort craft. A trio of A-wing starfighters play a crucial role in the battle, destroying Darth Vader's gigantic ship, the *Executor*.

SET HISTORY

	A-Wing Fighter Year 2006 Number 6207
	A-Wing Fighter Year 2000 Number 7134

Fusion reactor exhaust

Detachable engine block

Reinforced front can ram ships

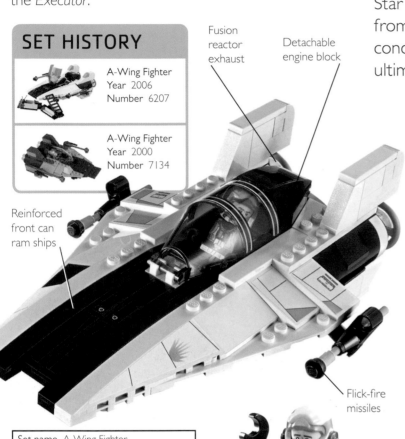

Flick-fire missiles

Set name A-Wing Fighter	
Year 2013	Number 75003
Pieces 177	Source EP IV & VI

Earlier A-wing minifigures wear a classic LEGO helmet, but the 2013 minifigure sports detailed, movie-accurate headgear and two faces.

A-WING PILOT

▼ Rebel Control Center

The rebels direct their forces at Endor from a mobile command center on board a massive Mon Calamari star cruiser. A-wings, B-wings, X-wings, and Y-wings are launched from hangars in the ship as well.

Repulsorlift crane

Set name B-Wing At Rebel Control Center	
Year 2000	Number 7180
Pieces 338	Source EP IV & VI

Battle of Endor

The Battle of Endor takes place on the surface of Endor's forest moon and in orbit around the planet. The Empire's second Death Star orbits the moon, protected by a defensive shield projected from a generator on the moon's surface. The rebels must concentrate all their resources on a concerted strike that will ultimately bring down the hated Empire.

▶ B-Wing Fighter

This B-wing model docks vertically at a service/refueling tower (regular B-wings land on their side with folded wings). The ship can deploy its S-foil wings for flight and its weapons are operated by flick-firing mechanisms.

SET HISTORY

	B-Wing at Rebel Control Center Year 2000 Number 7180

Set name B-Wing Fighter	
Year 2006	Number 6208
Pieces 435	Source EP IV & VI

Hinged cockpit canopy

Engine thrust nozzle

Energy cell for anti-gravity generator

Main wing

B-wing pilot Ten Numb

Maintenance platform

Targeting laser

Flight display monitor

Tool sled

Heavy laser cannon

Ewok Weapons

Endor's forest moon is inhabited by Ewoks, who help the rebels defeat the Imperial forces guarding the shield generator bunker (including, in this set, a stormtrooper and a scout trooper on a speeder bike). The Ewoks use weapons that are crude—simple wooden catapults and gliders—but these furry creatures are tough and resourceful.

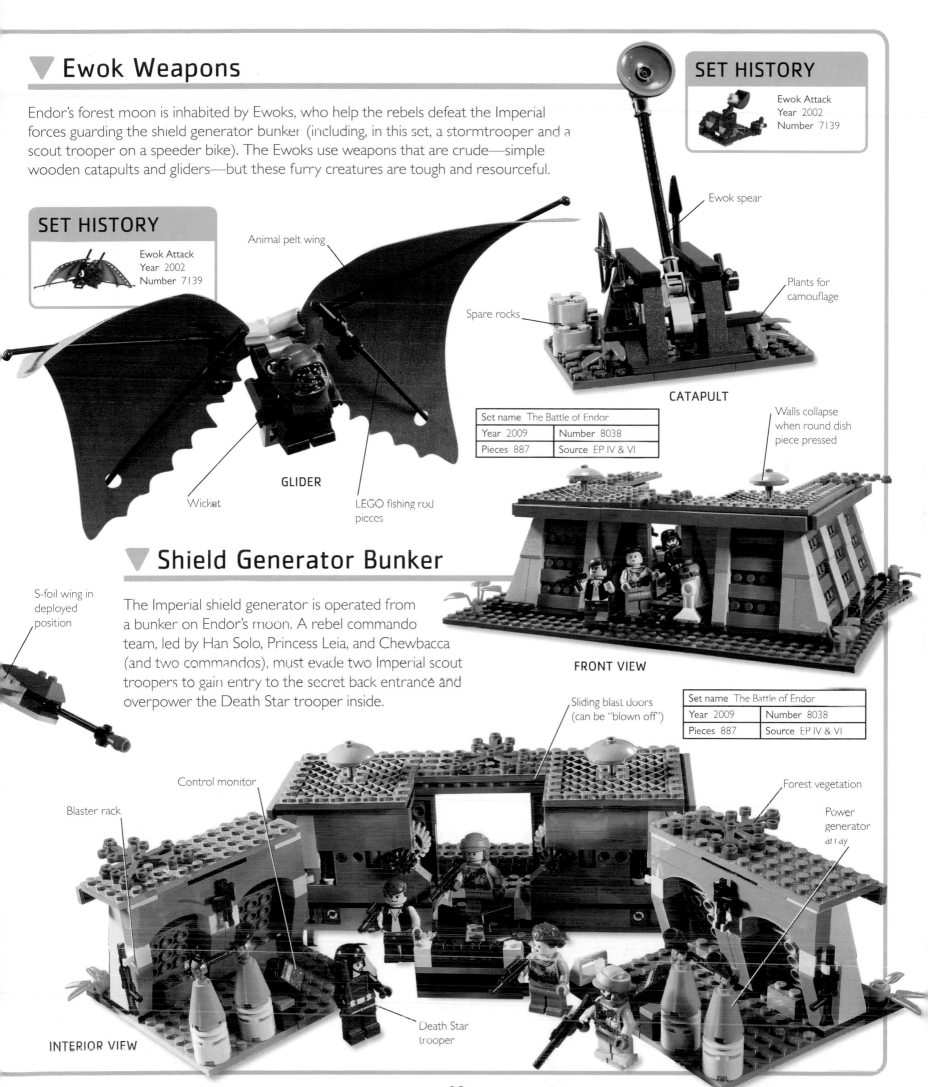

SET HISTORY

Ewok Attack
Year 2002
Number 7139

SET HISTORY

Ewok Attack
Year 2002
Number 7139

Ewok spear

Plants for camouflage

Spare rocks

CATAPULT

Animal pelt wing

Wicket

GLIDER

LEGO fishing rod pieces

Set name	The Battle of Endor	
Year 2009	Number 8038	
Pieces 887	Source EP IV & VI	

Walls collapse when round dish piece pressed

Shield Generator Bunker

S-foil wing in deployed position

The Imperial shield generator is operated from a bunker on Endor's moon. A rebel commando team, led by Han Solo, Princess Leia, and Chewbacca (and two commandos), must evade two Imperial scout troopers to gain entry to the secret back entrance and overpower the Death Star trooper inside.

FRONT VIEW

Sliding blast doors (can be "blown off")

Set name	The Battle of Endor	
Year 2009	Number 8038	
Pieces 887	Source EP IV & VI	

Control monitor

Blaster rack

Forest vegetation

Power generator array

Death Star trooper

INTERIOR VIEW

Bright Tree Village

Deep in the primeval woodland of Endor's forest moon is Bright Tree Village, the home of the Ewoks. Although the wooden building materials are primitive, the resourceful Ewoks have created a complex network of tree-top dwellings, protected by hidden fortifications. When the rebels stumble into Ewok territory, they get a mixed reception but soon win over the furry creatures— who prove to be an invaluable ally.

Minifigures can stand on tree branches

Foliage pieces used in the Naboo swamp set and Yoda's Hut on Dagobah

Vine lever controls crashing logs

Bendable tubes make guardrails

Flaming torches can be carried by minifigures

Princess Leia with flowing hair and dress

Luke with artificial hand

Rope bridge is detachable

Hidden trap door

Rare string pieces make up rope ladder

Printed mushroom

Exit chute for hidden trap door

DATA FILE

Set name: Ewok Village
Year: 2013   Set Number: 10236
Pieces: 1990   Source: EP IV–VI
Dimensions: length 55cm (21½in); depth 35cm (13¾in); height 35cm (13¾in)
Minifigures: 17 (Luke Skywalker, Han Solo, Princess Leia, Chewbacca, R2-D2, C-3PO, Wicket W. Warrick, Chief Chirpa, Logray, Teebo, Ewok Warrior, 2 rebel soldiers, 2 scout troopers, 2 stormtroopers)

▶ Ewoks

The five Ewoks in this set have more detailed printing than previous Ewok minifigures, for example, more elaborate bones and feathers, which the Ewoks adorn themselves with as hunting trophies.

Animal pelt hood

Stitching detail

WICKET W. WARRICK

Treetops rotate 360 degrees

Stocks for prisoners

Rocks for catapult

Canopy catapult

C-3PO's throne rises up

Winch for net

String to tie up prisoners

Imperial helmets used as drums

Forest produce

Hidden compartment in trunk

Net for booby trap

▲ Camp Fire

Han Solo finds himself on the menu for a banquet in C-3PO's honor. As the spit is turned, Han's minifigure brushes the flame pieces, creating the illusion of a flickering fire.

DIVINE DROID

The Ewoks proclaim C-3PO a god and reverentially carry him to their village. His throne fits onto the main set, where it can be raised on a clear rod, as though by Luke's command of the Force—or C-3PO's divine magic.

Metallic body not seen before by Ewoks

C-3PO'S LITTER

Steps lead to hidden room

Hunting spear

Gurreck skull

Staff of power

Bird skull

Bow

Animal pelt hood

Churri feather

Medicine bag

Animal tooth decoration

CHIEF CHIRPA

LOGRAY

EWOK WARRIOR

TEEBO

Stormtroopers, beware! Ewoks are masters of simple but effective engineering. A release mechanism causes two logs to smash together, taking out any attacking Imperial speeder bikes.

Ultimate Collector Sets

▼ TIE Interceptor

The TIE Interceptor is captured accurately, with its long dagger-like wings (which can be folded to lie flat) and a hinged cockpit with a detailed interior featuring a pilot seat, controls, a HUD (heads-up display or transparent data screen), and several monitor screens. The model sits on an adjustable stand, which allows it to be displayed in a variety of positions.

The LEGO Group has issued a small number of highly detailed *Star Wars* models called Ultimate Collector Sets (or UCS). Intended for older builders and primarily for display, each set includes a collector's card and, in many cases, a display stand. Most are not scaled for minifigures, though some, such as *Millennium Falcon*, are minifigure-scaled.

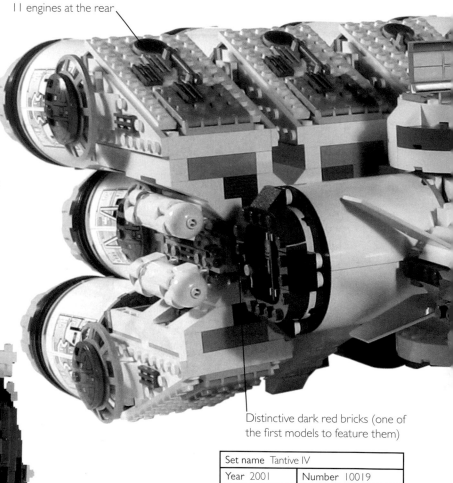

11 engines at the rear

Minimal use of blue elements

Modular, detachable wing

Wings 45cm (18in) long

Distinctive dark red bricks (one of the first models to feature them)

Set name	TIE Interceptor	
Year 2000	Number 7181	
Pieces 703	Source EP VI	

Set name	Tantive IV	
Year 2001	Number 10019	
Pieces 1748	Source EP IV	

▶ Darth Maul

The 45-cm (18-inch) tall bust of Sith apprentice Darth Maul has to be constructed from the bottom up and utilizes building techniques employed on expert models at LEGOLAND® Parks. This remarkably detailed model weighs almost 4 kg (9 lb).

Menacing eyes

▲ *Tantive IV*

Princess Leia Organa's consular starship, *Tantive IV* (otherwise known as the Blockade Runner), is one of the largest LEGO Ultimate Collector sets, at over 60cm (2 feet) long and almost 30cm (1 foot) wide. The highly detailed model is made up of separate sections—front, mid, and rear engine block—built individually and then pegged together. The top and lower turbo lasers rotate and the ship is supported on "landing gear" stands.

Bust can be supported on a special stand

Set name	Darth Maul	
Year 2001	Number 10018	
Pieces 1868	Source EP I	

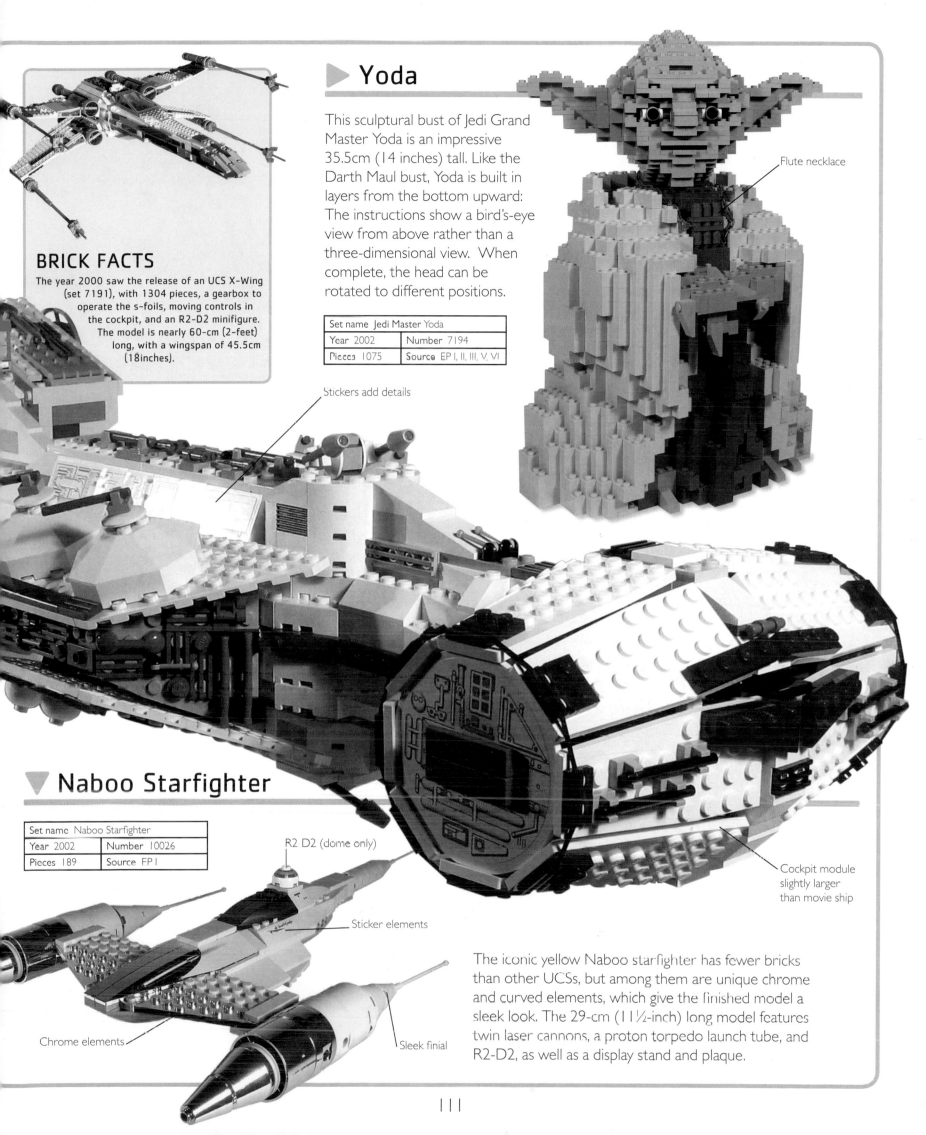

▶ Yoda

This sculptural bust of Jedi Grand Master Yoda is an impressive 35.5cm (14 inches) tall. Like the Darth Maul bust, Yoda is built in layers from the bottom upward: The instructions show a bird's-eye view from above rather than a three-dimensional view. When complete, the head can be rotated to different positions.

Flute necklace

Set name	Jedi Master Yoda	
Year 2002	Number 7194	
Pieces 1075	Source EP I, II, III, V, VI	

BRICK FACTS

The year 2000 saw the release of an UCS X-Wing (set 7191), with 1304 pieces, a gearbox to operate the s-foils, moving controls in the cockpit, and an R2-D2 minifigure. The model is nearly 60-cm (2-feet) long, with a wingspan of 45.5cm (18inches).

Stickers add details

▼ Naboo Starfighter

Set name	Naboo Starfighter	
Year 2002	Number 10026	
Pieces 189	Source EP I	

R2 D2 (dome only)

Sticker elements

Cockpit module slightly larger than movie ship

Chrome elements

Sleek finial

The iconic yellow Naboo starfighter has fewer bricks than other UCSs, but among them are unique chrome and curved elements, which give the finished model a sleek look. The 29-cm (11½-inch) long model features twin laser cannons, a proton torpedo launch tube, and R2-D2, as well as a display stand and plaque.

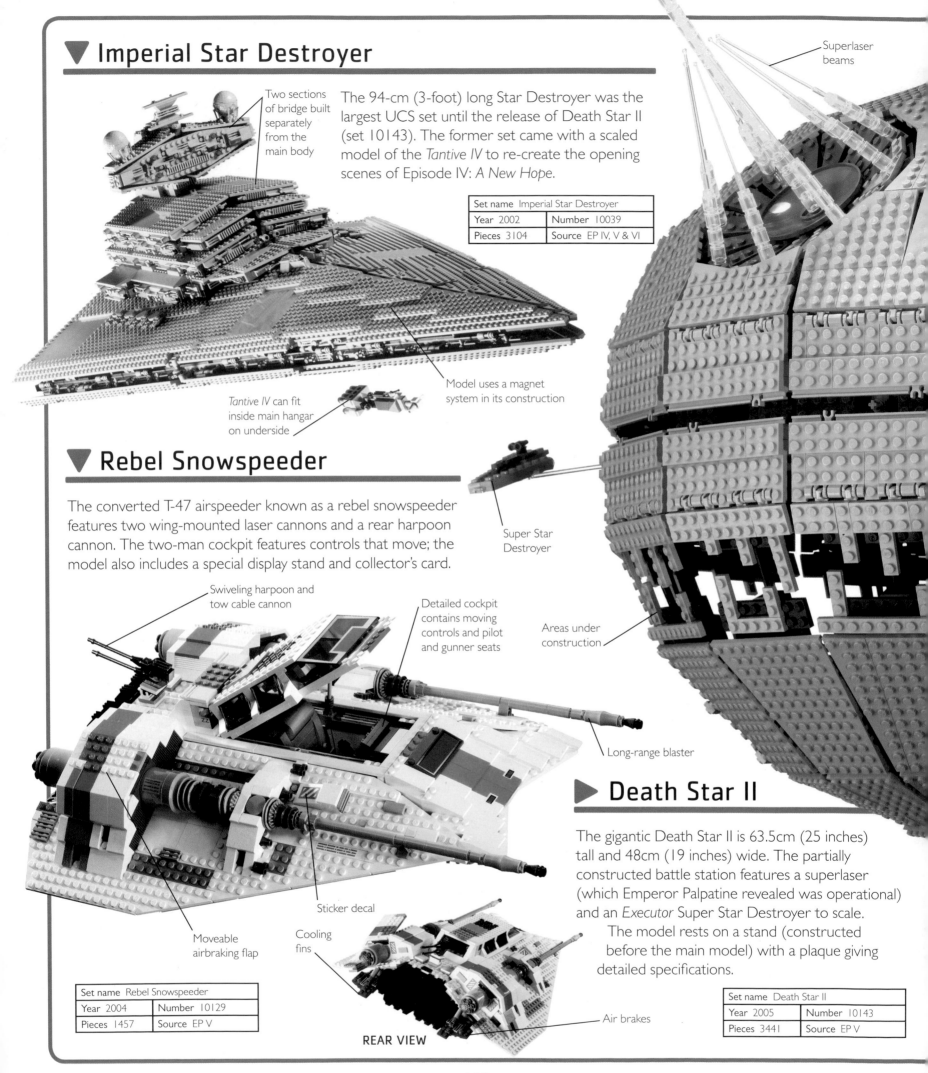

▼ Imperial Star Destroyer

Two sections of bridge built separately from the main body

The 94-cm (3-foot) long Star Destroyer was the largest UCS set until the release of Death Star II (set 10143). The former set came with a scaled model of the *Tantive IV* to re-create the opening scenes of Episode IV: *A New Hope*.

Set name	Imperial Star Destroyer	
Year 2002	Number 10039	
Pieces 3104	Source EP IV, V & VI	

Tantive IV can fit inside main hangar on underside

Model uses a magnet system in its construction

▼ Rebel Snowspeeder

The converted T-47 airspeeder known as a rebel snowspeeder features two wing-mounted laser cannons and a rear harpoon cannon. The two-man cockpit features controls that move; the model also includes a special display stand and collector's card.

Swiveling harpoon and tow cable cannon

Detailed cockpit contains moving controls and pilot and gunner seats

Super Star Destroyer

Long-range blaster

Sticker decal

Moveable airbraking flap

Cooling fins

Set name	Rebel Snowspeeder	
Year 2004	Number 10129	
Pieces 1457	Source EP V	

Air brakes

REAR VIEW

Superlaser beams

Areas under construction

▶ Death Star II

The gigantic Death Star II is 63.5cm (25 inches) tall and 48cm (19 inches) wide. The partially constructed battle station features a superlaser (which Emperor Palpatine revealed was operational) and an *Executor* Super Star Destroyer to scale.

The model rests on a stand (constructed before the main model) with a plaque giving detailed specifications.

Set name	Death Star II	
Year 2005	Number 10143	
Pieces 3441	Source EP V	

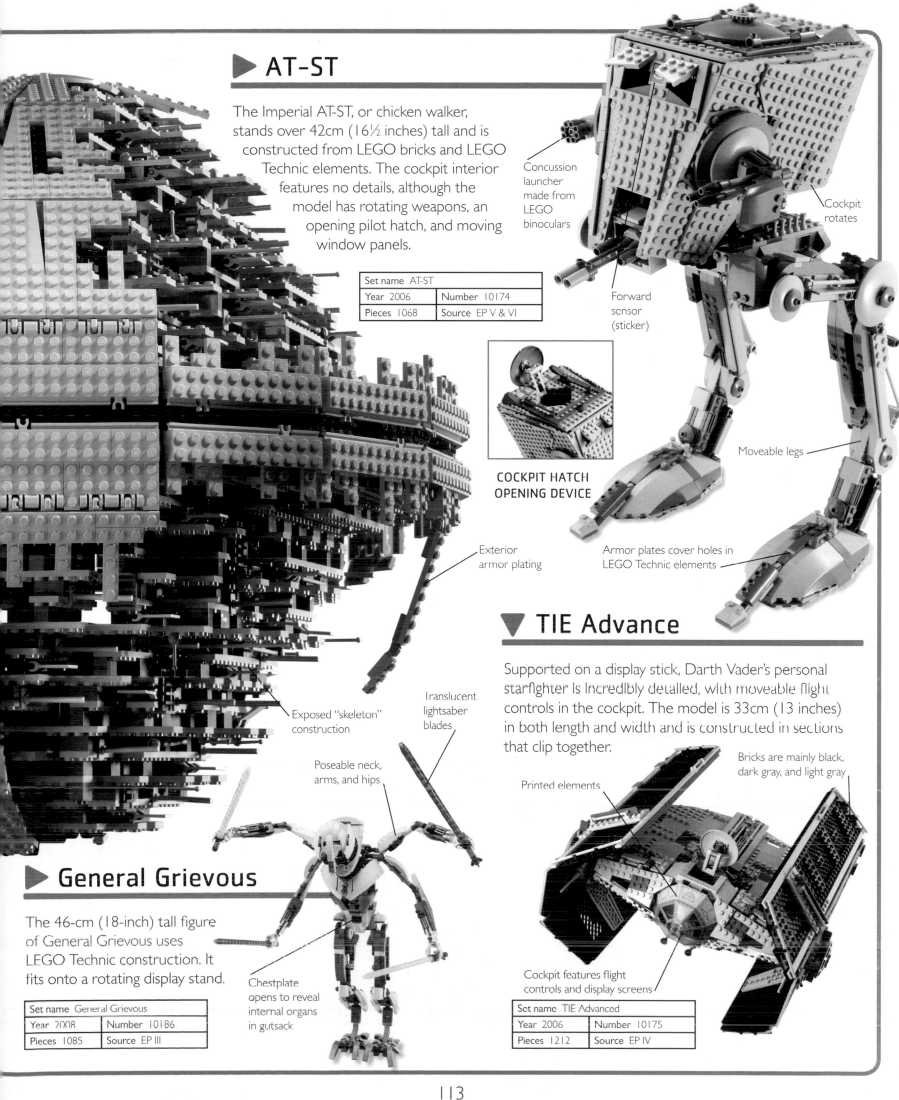

▶ AT-ST

The Imperial AT-ST, or chicken walker, stands over 42cm (16½ inches) tall and is constructed from LEGO bricks and LEGO Technic elements. The cockpit interior features no details, although the model has rotating weapons, an opening pilot hatch, and moving window panels.

Set name	AT-ST	
Year 2006		Number 10174
Pieces 1068		Source EP V & VI

Concussion launcher made from LEGO binoculars

Cockpit rotates

Forward sensor (sticker)

COCKPIT HATCH OPENING DEVICE

Moveable legs

Exterior armor plating

Armor plates cover holes in LEGO Technic elements

▼ TIE Advance

Supported on a display stick, Darth Vader's personal starfighter is incredibly detailed, with moveable flight controls in the cockpit. The model is 33cm (13 inches) in both length and width and is constructed in sections that clip together.

Bricks are mainly black, dark gray, and light gray

Printed elements

Translucent lightsaber blades

Poseable neck, arms, and hips

▶ General Grievous

The 46-cm (18-inch) tall figure of General Grievous uses LEGO Technic construction. It fits onto a rotating display stand.

Exposed "skeleton" construction

Chestplate opens to reveal internal organs in gutsack

Cockpit features flight controls and display screens

Set name	General Grievous	
Year 2008		Number 10186
Pieces 1085		Source EP III

Set name	TIE Advanced	
Year 2006		Number 10175
Pieces 1212		Source EP IV

Imperial Shuttle

The *Lambda*-class shuttle that carries Luke Skywalker from Endor to the Death Star measures 57cm (22 inches) wide with the wings unfolded and 71cm (28 inches) tall on its display stand. Keys at the rear raise and lower the wings, and the craft has landing gear that attaches to the bottom of the hull.

Navigation light

Reactor heat sink

OPEN COCKPIT

Wings fold up for landing

Rotating dual cannons

Cockpit holds four minifigures

Set name	Imperial Shuttle	
Year	2010	Number 10212
Pieces	2503	Film EP VI

Super Star Destroyer

The first-ever Super Star Destroyer produced by The LEGO Group is also the largest USC, measuring 124.5cm (50 inches) from bow to stern and weighing nearly 8lb (3.6kg). A section of the fuselage lifts up to reveal a command center where Darth Vader meets with bounty hunters searching for the *Millennium Falcon* (and takes orders from a unique, handheld hologram of the Emperor). A scaled version of the Imperial Star Destroyer connects to the hull with a clear rod.

Armored hull plates

Display stand

BOTTOM VIEW

Heavy laser cannon

Squadron markings

Obi-Wan's Jedi Starfighter

Obi-Wan Kenobi pursues bounty hunters across the galaxy in his Delta-7 *Aethersprite*-class light interceptor, which is 47cm (18 inches) long and 22cm (9 inches) wide when built. The Jedi starfighter has dual laser cannons and a fully detailed cockpit interior. The domed head of astromech droid R4-P17 attaches to the wing and rotates. The fighter also comes with a display stand and plaque.

Set name	Obi-Wan's Jedi Starfighter	
Year	2010	Number 10215
Pieces	676	Source EP II

Opening cockpit

Dual laser cannons

Communications transceiver

R4-P17

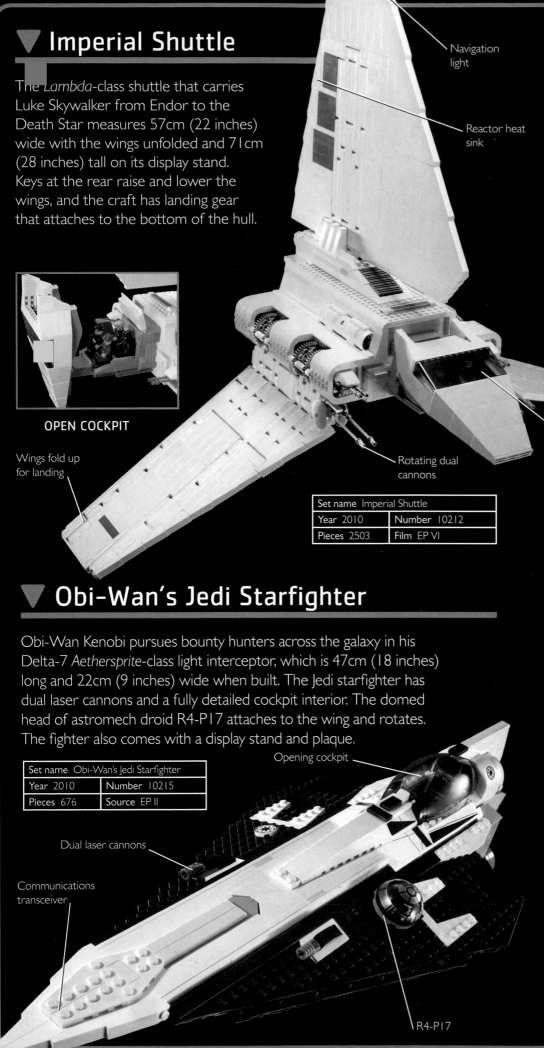

B-Wing Starfighter

A powerful strike fighter used by the rebels at the Battle of Endor, this B-wing measures 66cm (26 inches) wide and 38cm (15 inches) high. Its cockpit rotates and remains level in flight mode and its wings fold for takeoff and landing. Its designer decided on the scale by searching for parts for the cockpit, settling on motorcycle wheels and treads originally used in a LEGO bulldozer set from the 1970s.

Ion cannon

Set name	B-Wing Starfighter	
Year	2012	Number 10227
Pieces	1487	Source VI

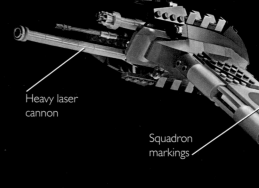

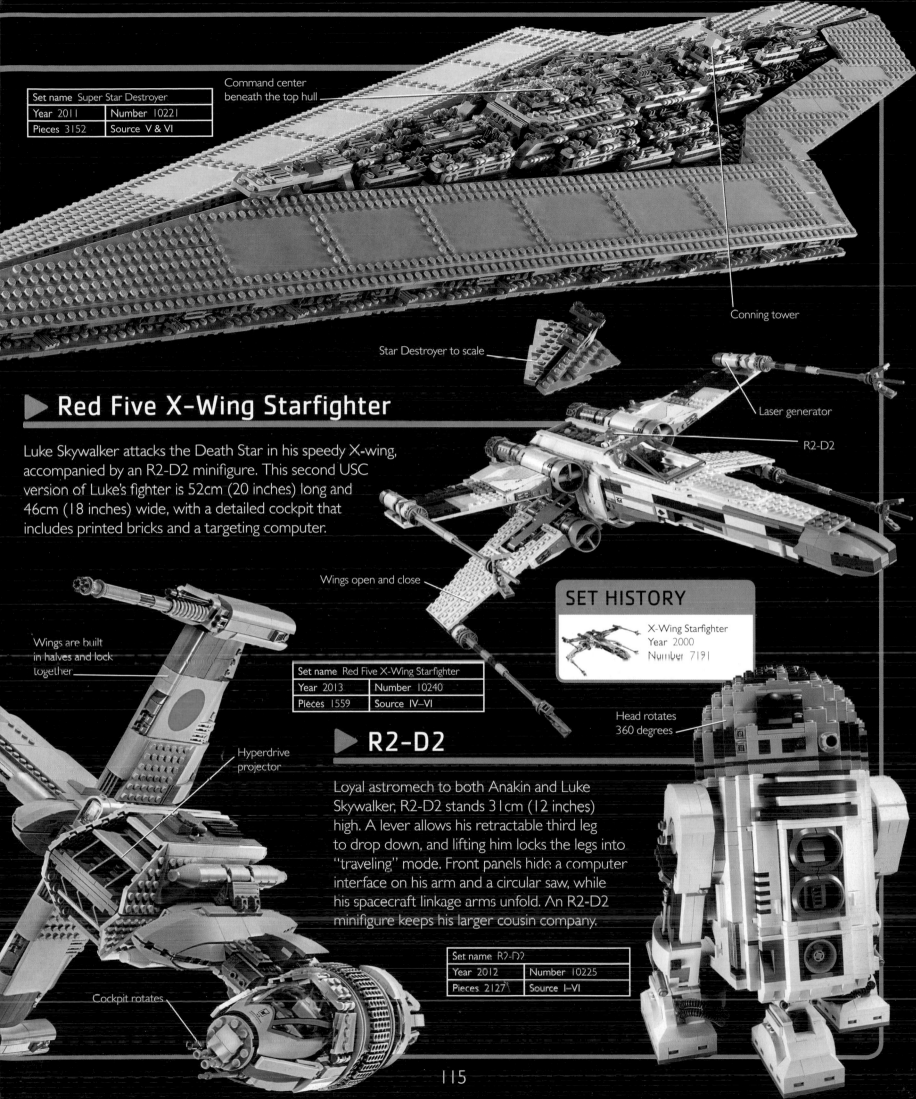

Set name	Super Star Destroyer	
Year 2011	Number 10221	
Pieces 3152	Source V & VI	

Command center
beneath the top hull

Conning tower

Star Destroyer to scale

Laser generator

R2-D2

▶ Red Five X-Wing Starfighter

Luke Skywalker attacks the Death Star in his speedy X-wing,
accompanied by an R2-D2 minifigure. This second USC
version of Luke's fighter is 52cm (20 inches) long and
46cm (18 inches) wide, with a detailed cockpit that
includes printed bricks and a targeting computer.

Wings open and close

Wings are built
in halves and lock
together

Hyperdrive
projector

Set name	Red Five X-Wing Starfighter	
Year 2013	Number 10240	
Pieces 1559	Source IV–VI	

SET HISTORY

X-Wing Starfighter
Year 2000
Number 7191

Head rotates
360 degrees

▶ R2-D2

Loyal astromech to both Anakin and Luke
Skywalker, R2-D2 stands 31cm (12 inches)
high. A lever allows his retractable third leg
to drop down, and lifting him locks the legs into
"traveling" mode. Front panels hide a computer
interface on his arm and a circular saw, while
his spacecraft linkage arms unfold. An R2-D2
minifigure keeps his larger cousin company.

Cockpit rotates

Set name	R2-D2	
Year 2012	Number 10225	
Pieces 2127	Source I–VI	

Seasonal Sets

Since 2011, the LEGO Group has released an annual seasonal set offering minifigures and parts for making micro sets of *Star Wars* vehicles. Children (or adults) open a window for each day of Advent for the countdown to Christmas, revealing a toy. Each seasonal set has surprises, such as a Christmas tree or a unique minifigure or two, dressed in garb appropriate for the holiday season.

▼ 2011 Advent Calendar

The countdown to Christmas 2011 began for LEGO fans with a miniature Republic cruiser and ended with Yoda resplendent in a Santa costume. Other highlights include a Republic gunship with movable wings, tools, and weapons racks, and a Christmas tree from a galaxy far, far away. The calendar art shows Yoda and a rebel pilot watching the Battle of Endor unfold around them.

Calendar window, complete with building instructions

Set name	2011 Advent Calendar	
Year 2011	Number 7958	
Pieces 266	Source EP I–VI	

Intergalactic Christmas tree

TIE Fighter pilot

Clone pilot

Homing spider droid

Slave I

R2-Q5

Snowspeeder

Chewbacca with bowcaster

JOLLY OLD ST. YODA
For Yoda, 800 years of life means many Jedi trained and many holidays delivering presents, like the two in his 2011 Advent Calendar backpack. Perhaps if Luke had stuck around on Dagobah he'd have found the candy cane from the Jedi Master's festive belt waiting in his stocking?

BRICK FACTS
Attendees of the 2011 San Diego Comic-Con could take home that year's advent calendar in special packaging telling them to open it by December 1. Only 1,000 were made.

2012 Advent Calendar

The LEGO Group's second festive *Star Wars* set has a snowy Hoth theme, with the box art showing a frozen pond on the planet's surface—perfect for skating. Exclusives include a Darth Maul minifigure in a Santa suit (with snowball), and an ingenious R2-D2 that looks like he's made out of snow, with a lump of coal for a radar eye, carrots for control arms, and even a top hat.

AT-AT Walker

Set name	2012 Advent Calendar	
Year	2012	Number 9509
Pieces	234	Source EP I–VI

Rebel trooper

Gungan soldier

Holiday Darth Maul

Snowman R2-D2

Flash Speeder

2013 Advent Calendar

For 2013, the spires of Geonosis were decorated with Christmas lights, and it was Jango Fett's turn to play Santa. Micro sets include Count Dooku's Solar Sailer, a Republic gunship that connects to an AT-TE walker, and a Coruscant freighter. Minifigures include R5-F7, an FA-4 pilot droid, and a bearded Endor rebel soldier.

Set name	2013 Advent Calendar	
Year	2013	Number 75023
Pieces	254	Source EP I–VI

Sprig of holly

JANGO BELLS
Jango Fett may not seem like a man filled with holiday cheer, but for the 2013 holidays he has left his Mandalorian sleigh on the rooftop, swapped his usual suit for a bright red one, and is armed with toys. Besides, it's a bounty hunter's job to know who's been naughty or nice.

HOLIDAY JANGO (DESCENDING CHIMNEY)

AIRSPEEDER

AT-TE

NEIMOIDIAN SHUTTLE

JEDI STARFIGHTER

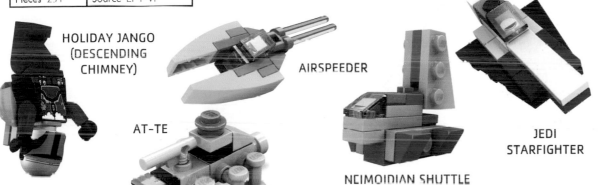

Merchandising

LEGO® *Star Wars*® is not just about bricks and pieces—fans can also dress the part and accessorize themselves (and their fridges) to match. Much of the LEGO *Star Wars* merchandise incorporates construction or play elements, such as watches you can build and customizable pens. Adult collectors can make grown-up-sized watches and special maquette minifigures—strictly for display, not play!

▶ Maquettes

California-based model-making company Gentle Giant Studios created a series of 15.25-cm (6-inch) limited-edition maquettes based on LEGO *Star Wars* videogame characters. As a surprise extra, some Vader maquettes came with a spare gray Anakin Skywalker head and a few stormtroopers also had a Han Solo head!

▶ Key Chains

If you want to keep safe the keys to your starfighter, then these key chains are just what you need! Characters available include Watto, Admiral Ackbar, Darth Vader, and Yoda.

BLACKHOLE TROOPER (2007)

Maquettes made of polyresin

STORMTROOPER (2007)

Poseable, removeable head held on with magnets

BOBA FETT (2007)

DARTH VADER (2007)

Key chain can also be used as a backpack charm

WATTO (2012)

ADMIRAL ACKBAR (2010)

BIKER SCOUT (2012)

Bag Charms

JEDI STARFIGHTER™
Exclusive Bag Charm

Ages/
edades
6+

Bigger than key chains, bag charms feature minivehicles rather than minifigures. Choose from a Jedi starfighter, a Y-wing starfighter, Luke Skywalker's landspeeder, Darth Vader's TIE fighter, *Slave I*, or the *Millennium Falcon*.

Key Lights

Arms and legs are poseable

If you find yourself leaning toward the dark side, brighten things up with this fun Darth Vader light key chain. Push buttons activate two bright LED lights that shoot out powerful beams from the evil Lord's feet.

Watches

LEGO *Star Wars* watches are available in child and adult sizes. Like a LEGO model, they must be built: Strap links are snapped together in any combination then joined to the face and clasp.

Strap links

LEGO minifigure on face

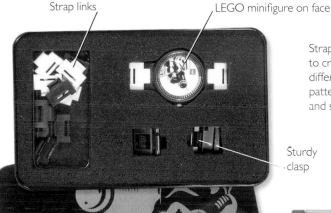

Decorative tin

STORMTROOPER
ADULT WATCH (2009)

Luke Skywalker minifigure

Strap links to create different patterns and sizes

Sturdy clasp

50m/165ft

LUKE SKYWALKER
WATCH (2007)

DARTH VADER
WATCH (2013)

Watch comes with a Darth Vader minifigure that can be fixed onto the watch strap

Magnets

You will never lose the secret Death Star plans if you stick them to the fridge door with one of these extra cool minifigure magnets. Characters available include Princess Leia, complete with blaster gun, and various characters from *Star Wars: The Clone Wars* animations.

Figures are not detachable from their LEGO brick base

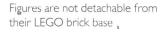

AURRA SING, EMBO, AND AN ARF TROOPER (2012)

Ages/edades
6+

PRINCESS LEIA™
Magnet · Aimant · Imán

PRINCESS LEIA
(2013)

Promotional Pieces

All around the world, LEGO® *Star Wars®* fans get together in small venues and giant convention centers to learn the latest LEGO news, share their creations, and encourage fellow builders. The LEGO Group often attends these events to showcase new sets and interact with its enthusiastic builders and collectors. Loyal fans are often rewarded with exclusive LEGO *Star Wars* sets or minifigures—the space race to locate collectible promotional items is on!

▶ Rare Minifigures

To celebrate 30 years of the LEGO minifigure, 10,000 metallic gold C-3PO minifigures were randomly inserted into LEGO *Star Wars* sets in 2007. Even rarer are the five C-3PO minifigures made of solid 14kt gold! In 2010 Boba Fett joined the highest ranks of exclusivity when two solid bronze variants were released as part of a "May the Fourth" promotion. That year also saw 10,000 white Bobas given away at toy fairs and *Star Wars* Days.

▼ Life-Size X-Wing in Times Square

To celebrate the May 2013 launch of the new animated TV series *The Yoda Chronicles*, the LEGO Group unveiled a life-sized X-wing (scaled for humans rather than minifigures) in Times Square, New York. The build is an exact replica of the X-Wing Starfighter (set 9493), magnified 42 times, and consisting of 5,335,200 LEGO bricks. It took a team of 32 builders 17,336 hours (about 4 months) to construct and is officially the world's largest ever LEGO model. The event also included a LEGO R2-D2 and X-wing pilot model ready for photo opportunities, and a LEGO Yoda bearing a t-shirt with the slogan "NY I Love."

The X-wing builders had to make sure that their model, weighing 20,856kg (45,980lb), would be safe above the New York subway system!

The super-sized starfighter measures 3.35m (11ft) in height, 13.1m (43ft) in length, and has a wingspan of 13.44m (44ft).

The model was carefully built to withstand transportation—from its original base in the LEGO Model Shop in Kladno, Czech Republic, to New York, and finally on to LEGOLAND® California.

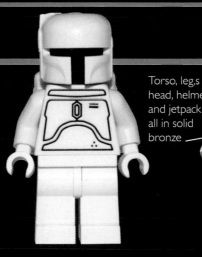

Engraved chest detailing

Torso, legs, head, helmet, and jetpack all in solid bronze

Printed torso pattern

CHROME GOLD C-3PO
(2007)

SOLID GOLD C-3PO
(2007)

WHITE BOBA FETT
(2010)

SOLID BRONZE BOBA FETT
(2010)

▼ Comic-Con Exclusives

Annual comic-con events have undergone a massive surge in popularity in recent years. The LEGO Group has a big presence at these gatherings, where they often hand out or sell exclusive promotional sets or minifigures. This range displays some of the recent microfighter giveaways—revealed before the launch of the 2014 Microfighter line.

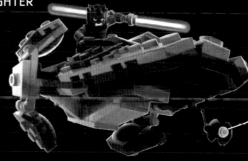

Only 1000 produced, packaged in a special metal cube

Movable wings

Exclusive Boba minifigure

SAN DIEGO COMIC-CON
JEK-14 STEALTH STARFIGHTER
(2013)

STAR WARS CELEBRATION VI
BOBA FETT'S MINI *SLAVE 1*
(2007)

Available to the first 200 customers on each day of the 2012 New York Comic-Con

Giveaway also included a Sith probe droid

Exclusive Luke Skywalker minifigure

NEW YORK COMIC-CON
LUKE'S LANDSPEEDER
(2012)

SAN DIEGO COMIC-CON
SITH INFILTRATOR
(2012)

▼ New York Toy Fair Exclusives

In 2005, at the New York Toy Fair, attendees of the LEGO Group's V.I.P. gala event received a special edition of the Darth Vader transformation set, packaged inside a special slipcase.

At the 2009 New York Toy Fair, lucky guests received a chrome Darth Vader minifigure in an exclusive box.

Fan Creations

The LEGO® fan community spans generations, reaches across continents, and bridges languages. The beauty of LEGO bricks is that you can make just about anything with them, and groups of expert builders, or AFOLS (Adult Fans of LEGO), do just that. Their custom designs even have their own specialist term: MOCs (My Own Creations). The simple brick has been transformed into the most creative and versatile construction element in the world.

▶ Carbon-Freezing Chamber

Markus Aspacher (markus1984) took just five days to create this wonderful MOC of the Carbon-Freezing Chamber in 2013. Measuring 34 x 40 centimeters (13 x 16 inches), it utilizes around 2000 bricks. A Han Solo minifigure being lowered into the freezing chamber brings the whole grisly scene to life.

▶ Mos Eisley

The Brickish Association is a UK-based community of AFOLS. Its members displayed their impressively detailed Mos Eisley diorama at the UK's National Space Centre and at *Star Wars: Celebration Europe* in 2007.

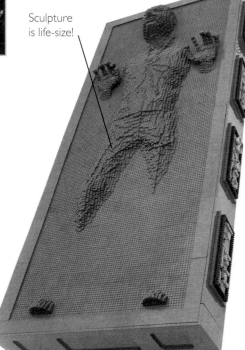

12 people built and contributed buildings, vehicles, and figures

A Boba Fett minifigure watches over the scene

Many movie-accurate details (these stormtroopers are searching for missing droids)

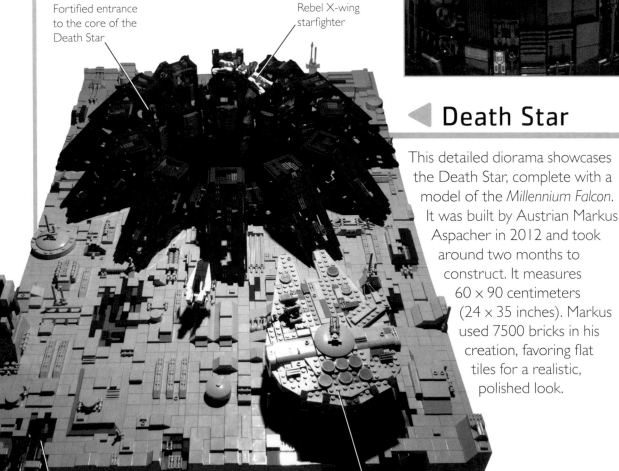

Fortified entrance to the core of the Death Star

Rebel X-wing starfighter

"Unfinished" section of hull represented by red bricks.

Detailed model of the *Millennium Falcon*

◀ Death Star

This detailed diorama showcases the Death Star, complete with a model of the *Millennium Falcon*. It was built by Austrian Markus Aspacher in 2012 and took around two months to construct. It measures 60 x 90 centimeters (24 x 35 inches). Markus used 7500 bricks in his creation, favoring flat tiles for a realistic, polished look.

Sculpture is life-size!

▲ Frozen Han Solo

Artist and brick builder extraordinaire Nathan Sawaya used 10,000 bricks to create this 1.7-meter (5.5-feet) tall sculpture of Han Solo frozen in carbonite.

Model of the crashed starship Dowager Queen

Some of the landspeeders are motorized

50 LEDs light the interior

Tan-colored bricks were collected over many years, many from LEGO Adventurers "Egypt" sets

Echo Base

Mark Borlase's re-creation of Echo Base took four years to build. It has motorized hangar doors, a *Millennium Falcon*, and superbly detailed AT-ATs. Snowtroopers lower themselves from AT-ATs and advance toward the rebel lines, complete with laser turrets and tauntauns.

Theed Hangar

Amado C. Pinlac (ACPin) has been building impressive MOCs for over a decade. This wonderfully detailed diorama captures the Theed hangar battle scene, and includes four N-1 starfighters and an advancing Trade Federation droid army. The scene took Amado three months to build.

Obi-Wan and Qui-Gon Jinn battle Darth Maul

Anakin Skywalker takes off in an N-1 Naboo starfighter

CAMP FIRE ON TATOOINE

THE BATTLE OF HOTH

FAN ART
South Korean photographer Jo Hyung Lee (storm TK431) creates imaginative images using his own backgrounds and a variety of LEGO *Star Wars* minifigures. The scenes have a modern, humorous twist, so don't be surprised if you see a stormtrooper-versus-Jedi ice-hockey match, or stormtroopers playing guitar and toasting marshmallows around a campfire!

Video Games

In 2005 the LEGO® *Star Wars*® minifigure boldly went where it hadn't been before. LEGO *Star Wars: The Video Game* enabled gamers to play through the action of Episodes I–III as any one of 56 minifigures, from Obi-Wan Kenobi to a GNK Droid! It was followed in 2006 by LEGO *Star Wars II: The Original Trilogy* and in 2011 by LEGO *Star Wars III: The Clone Wars*.

▼ A World of Adventure

Yoda storms into battle flanked by loyal clone troopers in LEGO *Star Wars III: The Clone Wars*.

When TT Games and the LEGO Group developed the digital version of LEGO *Star Wars*, they wanted the functionality of the games to match the physical playability of the sets that fans know and love. So, gamers can play from the viewpoint of various minifigure characters, and LEGO studs act as the games' currency—to be collected while wandering around the interactive levels.

Players can freeze one character and swap to another. Here, the action is switching from Anakin to Ahsoka.

▼ Into Space

As well as playing as minifigures, the digital world allows gamers to control spaceships and, on a grander scale, fly some of the most iconic LEGO *Star Wars* craft. In LEGO *Star Wars II: The Original Trilogy,* you can unlock *Slave I* and achieve every wannabe-pilot's dream: pilot an X-wing to destroy the Death Star itself!

▼ Brick by Brick

The digital LEGO world presents lifelike building challenges. See a pile of bricks? Wait whilst your on-screen minifigure assembles them into a recognizable LEGO *Star Wars* structure before progressing farther.

BUILD YOUR OWN
Highlighting the humorous and fun aspects of LEGO playability, after unlocking all characters, you can customize minifigures and give them a whole new look. Fancy playing as Slave Girl Vader? Now you can!

TV Specials

If the interactive video games brought the LEGO® Star Wars® theme to life, then in 2009, the animated TV special introduced R2-D2 and all his LEGO minifigure friends to the big screen. The humor and fun of these "shorts" continues to go from strength to strength.

▶ The Quest for R2-D2

To celebrate 10 highly successful years of the LEGO Star Wars line, Lucasfilm and the LEGO Group came together in 2009 to produce their first ever short film. As the title suggests, The Quest for R2-D2 makes a certain LEGO droid its star player as he is lost, found, and makes a female astromech friend. There is even a cameo appearance from a LEGO Indiana Jones.

The five minutes of animated LEGO fun premiered on Cartoon Network.

▼ The Empire Strikes Out

A gleeful Sith Lord accidentally blasts his young apprentice with Force lightning.

Father-son issues are a familiar theme in Star Wars, but the 2012 episode The Empire Strikes Out takes this to whole new levels. In it, Darth Vader and Darth Maul squabble for their Master's attentions, while Death Star destroyer Luke Skywalker is hounded across the galaxy by besotted fangirls.

▼ Bombad Bounty

In his starring role, Jar Jar starts out mopping the ship floor, inadvertently causing Darth Vader to slip up!

Following on from The Quest for R2-D2, 2010 saw the release of its sequel Bombad Bounty. The five minute-long comedic episode follows Boba Fett and Jar Jar Binks, and plays homage to many other popular films.

▼ The Padawan Menace

Young Padawans are treated to a tour of Coruscant before chaos breaks out!

Yoda and Asajj Ventress engage in a duel, during which Asajj is sliced in half—only to reassemble her LEGO parts and carry on!

Featuring familiar voices from the Star Wars: The Clone Wars TV series, the 30-minute long animation The Padawan Menace appeared on TV screens in 2011. The script featured in-jokes crossing over from episodes I–VI, and was also the animated episode to introduce the world to the young and mischievous minifigure "Ian"—otherwise known as Han Solo—and a minifigure version of George Lucas himself.

▼ The Yoda Chronicles

The Yoda Chronicles is set in the Prequel years, with an emphasis on the conflict between good and evil.

Having progressed from five to thirty minutes in length, the first episode of a LEGO Star Wars TV trilogy launched in 2013. The Yoda Chronicles "The Phantom Clone" aired in 2013, followed by "Menace of the Sith," and concluding with "Attack of the Jedi"— with more episodes to follow in 2014. The mini-series focuses on Grand Master Yoda, and also introduces the lone clone JEK-14.

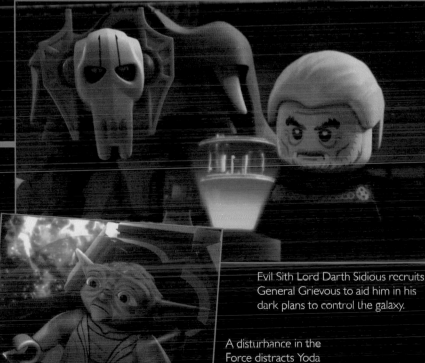

Evil Sith Lord Darth Sidious recruits General Grievous to aid him in his dark plans to control the galaxy.

A disturbance in the Force distracts Yoda from training Padawans.

Minifigure Gallery

The vast collection of LEGO® Star Wars® minifigures features imaginative molds and accessories, some of which were specially designed for the unique characters and species found in the Star Wars universe. The basic LEGO minifigure arrives for the builder to assemble in three sections: a head; a torso (with and arms and hands); and hips and legs. Many Star Wars minifigures also include exciting extras, such as helmets, interesting hair pieces, and of course, lightsabers!

Anakin Skywalker (1999)

Anakin Skywalker (1999)

Anakin Skywalker (2007)

Anakin Skywalker (2011)

Anakin Skywalker (2011)

Anakin Skywalker (2002)

Anakin Skywalker (2002)

Anakin Skywalker (2013)

Anakin Skywalker (2010)

Anakin Skywalker (2005)

Anakin Skywalker (2005)

Anakin Skywalker (2008)

Anakin Skywalker (2011)

Anakin Skywalker (2014)

Anakin Skywalker (2014)

Anakin Skywalker (2012)

Anakin Skywalker (2012)

Anakin Skywalker (2005)

Anakin Skywalker (2010)

Darth Vader (1999)

Darth Vader (2005)

Darth Vader (2005)

Darth Vader (2008)

Darth Vader (2008)

Darth Vader (2009)

Darth Vader (2013)

Darth Vader (2014)

Darth Vader (2008)

Qui-Gon Jinn (1999)

Qui-Gon Jinn (2007)

Qui-Gon Jinn (2007)

Qui-Gon Jinn (2011)

Qui-Gon Jinn (2012)

Obi-Wan Kenobi (2002)

Obi-Wan Kenobi (2012)

Obi-Wan Kenobi (1999)

Obi-Wan Kenobi (2005)

Obi-Wan Kenobi (2007)

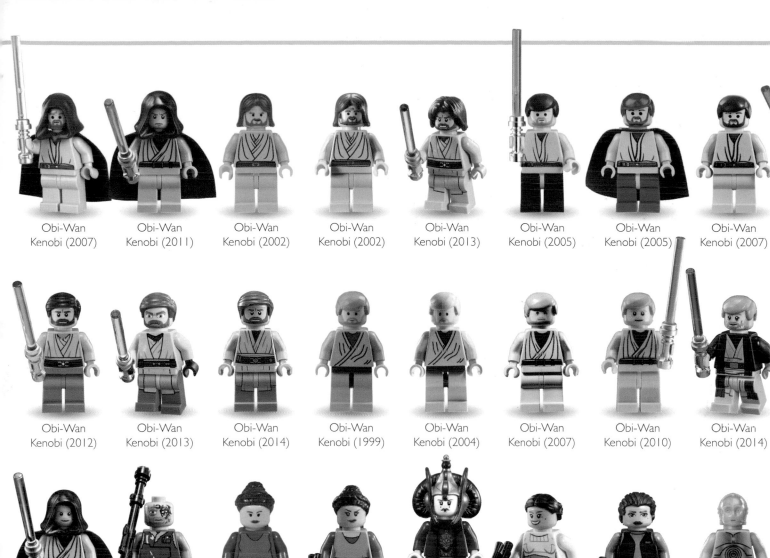

Obi-Wan Kenobi (2007)   Obi-Wan Kenobi (2011)   Obi-Wan Kenobi (2002)   Obi-Wan Kenobi (2002)   Obi-Wan Kenobi (2013)   Obi-Wan Kenobi (2005)   Obi-Wan Kenobi (2005)   Obi-Wan Kenobi (2007)   Obi-Wan Kenobi (2008)

Obi-Wan Kenobi (2012)   Obi-Wan Kenobi (2013)   Obi-Wan Kenobi (2014)   Obi-Wan Kenobi (1999)   Obi-Wan Kenobi (2004)   Obi-Wan Kenobi (2007)   Obi-Wan Kenobi (2010)   Obi-Wan Kenobi (2014)   Obi-Wan Kenobi (2008)

Obi-Wan Kenobi (2011)   Obi-Wan Kenobi (2013)   Padmé Naberrie (1999)   Padmé Naberrie (2011)   Queen Amidala (2012)   Padmé Amidala (2013)   Padmé Amidala (2012)   C-3PO (2000)   C-3PO (2005)

C-3PO (2008)   C-3PO (2012)   C-3PO (2014)   C-3PO (2007)   K-3PO (2007)   Protocol Droid (2008)   R-3PO (2011)   TC-14 Protocol Droid (2012)   R2-D2 (1999)

R2-D2 (2008)   R2-D2 (2009)   R2-D2 (2014)   R2-D2 (2006)   R2-D2 (2013)   R2-D2 (2012)   R2-D5 (2006)   R2-Q2 (2011)   R2-Q5 (2008)

 R2-R7
(2007)

 R2 Unit
(2014)

 R3-D5
(2012)

 R4-G0
(2013)

 R4-P17
(2013)

 R4-P17
(2014)

 R4-P44
(2010)

 R5-D4
(1999)

 R5-D4
(2005)

 R5-D4
(2014)

 R5-D8
(2012)

 R5-F7
(2012)

 R5-J2
(2012)

 R7-A7
(2009)

 R7-D4
(2010)

 R8-B7
(2011)

 Aldar Beedo
(2001)

 Sebulba
(1999)

 Sebulba
(2011)

 Watto
(2001)

 Watto
(2011)

 Wald
(2011)

 Captain Panaka
(2011)

 Naboo Security
Officer (2000)

 Naboo Fighter
Pilot (2007)

 Naboo Fighter
Pilot (2011)

 Jar Jar Binks
(1999)

 Jar Jar Binks
(2011)

 Gungan Soldier
(2000)

 Gungan Soldier
(2011)

 Republic Pilot
(2007)

 Republic
Captain (2007)

 Count Dooku
(2002)

 Count Dooku
(2009)

Count Dooku
(2013)

Chancellor
Palpatine (2009)

 Chancellor
Palpatine (2012)

 Chancellor
Palpatine (2014)

 Emperor
Palpatine (2000)

 Emperor
Palpatine (2005)

 Emperor
Palpatine (2008)

 Darth Maul
(1999)

 Darth Maul
(2011)

 Darth Maul
(2012)

 Santa Darth
Maul (2012)

Darth Maul
(2013)

Yoda
(2002)

Yoda
(2009)

Yoda
(2013)

Santa Yoda
(2011)

Tusken Raider
(2002)

Zam Wesell
(2002)

Jango Fett
(2002)

Jango Fett
(2013)

Jango Fett
(2013)

Boba Fett
(2002)

Boba Fett
(2013)

Boba Fett
(2006)

Boba Fett
(2003)

Boba Fett
(2009)

Boba Fett
(2010)

Boba Fett
(2012)

Boba Fett
(2010)

Phase 1 Clone
Trooper (2002)

Phase 1 Clone
Trooper (2008)

Phase 1 Clone
Trooper (2008)

Phase 1 Clone
Trooper (2008)

Phase 1 Clone
Trooper (2010)

Phase 1 Clone
Trooper (2013)

Phase 1 Clone
Trooper (2011)

Phase 1 Clone
Trooper
Sergeant (2013)

Clone Trooper
Lieutenant
(2013)

Clone Trooper
Captain (2013)

Clone
Commander
(2009)

Clone
Commander
(2010)

Clone Trooper
Commander
(2013)

Captain Rex
(2008)

Captain Rex
(2011)

Captain Rex
(2013)

Commander
Cody (2008)

Commander
Cody (2011)

Commander
Fox (2008)

Clone
Commander
Wolffe (2011)

Clone
Commander
Gree (2012)

Clone
Commander
Gree (2014)

Clone Jet
Trooper (2009)

Clone Gunner
(2009)

Wolfpack Clone
Trooper (2011)

Bomb Squad
Trooper (2011)

Phase 1 Clone
Pilot (2008)

Phase 1 Clone
Pilot (2013)

Shadow ARF
Trooper (2011)

ARF Trooper
(2011)

ARC Trooper
(2012)

Phase II Clone
Trooper (2005)

Phase II Clone
Trooper (2005)

Phase II Clone
Trooper (2005)

Phase II Clone
Trooper (2005)

Phase II Clone
Trooper (2010)

Phase II Clone
Trooper (2014)

Utapau Trooper
(2014)

Utapau Trooper
(2014)

Kashyyyk
Trooper (2014)

Commander
Neyo (2014)

Scout Trooper
(2005)

Scout Trooper
(2014)

Star Corps
Trooper (2005)

Star Corps
Trooper (2007)

Shock Trooper
(2007)

Shock Trooper
(2008)

Shock Trooper
(2014)

ARC Trooper
(2012)

501st Legion
Clone Trooper
(2013)

212th Clone
Trooper (2013)

Wolf Trooper
(2014)

Clone Pilot
(2005)

Clone Pilot
(2010)

Clone Pilot
(2010)

Clone Pilot
(2010)

Phase II Clone
Pilot (2014)

501st Clone
Pilot (2013)

Jedi Knight
(2002)

Mace Windu
(2005)

Mace Windu
(2006)

Mace Windu
(2009)

Mace Windu
(2012)

Mace Windu
(2013)

Coleman Trebor
(2013)

Agen Kolar
(2012)

Luminara Unduli
(2005)

Luminara Unduli
(2011)

Barriss Offee
(2010)

Barriss Offee
(2012)

Eeth Koth
(2011)

Even Piell
(2012)

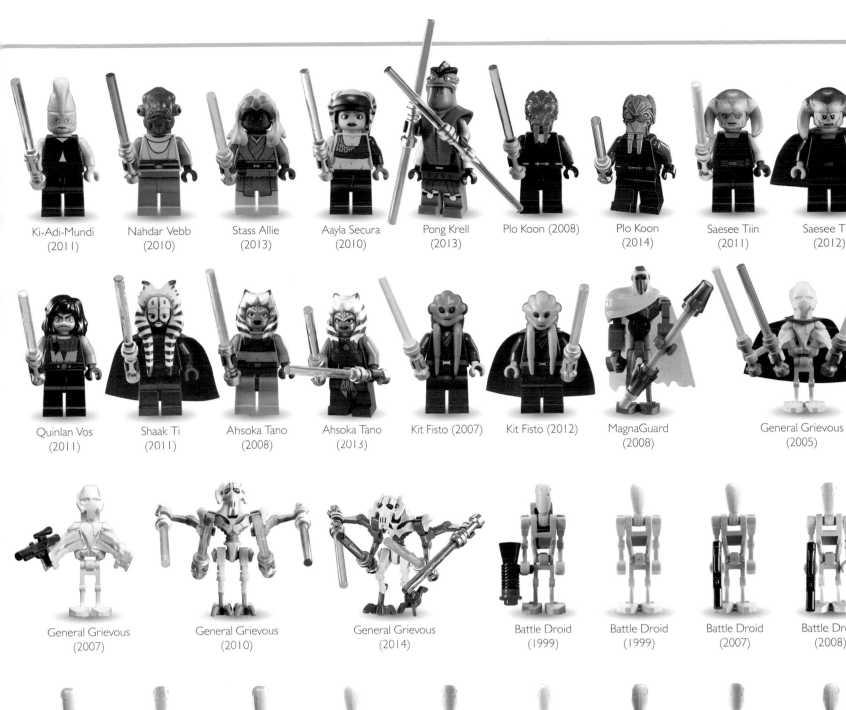

Ki-Adi-Mundi
(2011)

Nahdar Vebb
(2010)

Stass Allie
(2013)

Aayla Secura
(2010)

Pong Krell
(2013)

Plo Koon (2008)

Plo Koon
(2014)

Saesee Tiin
(2011)

Saesee Tiin
(2012)

Quinlan Vos
(2011)

Shaak Ti
(2011)

Ahsoka Tano
(2008)

Ahsoka Tano
(2013)

Kit Fisto (2007)

Kit Fisto (2012)

MagnaGuard
(2008)

General Grievous
(2005)

General Grievous
(2007)

General Grievous
(2010)

General Grievous
(2014)

Battle Droid
(1999)

Battle Droid
(1999)

Battle Droid
(2007)

Battle Droid
(2008)

Battle Droid
Commander
(2000)

Battle Droid
Commander
(2008)

Battle Droid
Commander
(2012)

Battle Droid
Pilot (2001)

Battle Droid
Pilot (2009)

Battle Droid
Pilot (2009)

Battle Droid
(2011)

Battle Droid
Pilot (2011)

Security Battle
Droid (2002)

Security Battle
Droid (2007)

Security Battle
Droid (2011)

Battle Droid
Geonosian
(2003)

Rocket Battle
Droid (2009)

Rocket Droid
Commander
(2010)

Battle Droid
(2013)

Battle Droid
Commander
(2013)

Commando
Droid (2012)

Commando
Droid Captain
(2013)

Greedo
(2004)

Greedo
(2014)

Bith
(2014)

Jawa
(2005)

Jawa
(2014)

Jawa
(2014)

Imperial Officer
(2014)

Imperial Officer
(2002)

Imperial Officer
(2005)

Imperial Officer
(2006)

Imperial Officer
(2010)

Imperial Officer
(2012)

Imperial Officer
(2014)

Admiral Piett
(2011)

Imperial Officer
(2014)

General Veers
(2007)

General Veers
(2010)

General Veers
(2014)

Imperial Officer
(2010)

Imperial Officer
(2012)

Grand Moff
Tarkin (2006)

Imperial Shuttle
Pilot (2001)

Imperial Pilot
(2010)

Imperial AT-ST
Pilot (2007)

Imperial AT-ST
Driver (2012)

Imperial V-Wing
Pilot (2011)

TIE Fighter Pilot
(2001)

TIE Fighter Pilot
(2012)

TIE Bomber
Pilot (2013)

TIE Defender
Pilot (2010)

TIE Interceptor
Pilot (2014)

Death Star
Trooper (2012)

Death Star
Trooper (2014)

Death Star
Trooper (2014)

Imperial
Trooper (2014)

Stormtrooper
(2005)

Stormtrooper
(2006)

Stormtrooper
(2007)

Stormtrooper
(2007)

Stormtrooper
(2009)

Stormtrooper
(2010)

Stormtrooper
(2012)

Stormtrooper
(2014)

Sandtrooper
(2012)

Sandtrooper
(2014)

138

AT-AT Driver (2007)   AT-AT Driver (2010)   AT-AT Driver (2014)   Snowtrooper (2007)   Snowtrooper (2012)   Snowtrooper (2013)   Snowtrooper (2014)   Scout Trooper (1999)   Scout Trooper (2012)

Scout Trooper (2013)   Royal Guard (2001)   Royal Guard (2008)   Royal Guard (2014)   Han Solo (2011)   Han Solo (2000)   Han Solo (2004)   Han Solo (2011)   Han Solo (2014)

Han Solo (2000)   Han Solo (2007)   Han Solo (2013)   Han Solo (2008)   Han Solo (2011)   Han Solo (2004)   Han Solo (2004)   Han Solo (2006)   Han Solo (2009)

Han Solo (2011)   Han Solo (2013)   Han Solo (2000)   Han Solo (2006)   Han Solo (2010)   Han Solo (2012)   Admiral Ackbar (2009)   Mon Calamari Officer (2009)   Mon Mothma (2009)

Captain Antilles (2009)   Crix Madine (2009)   Crix Madine (2009)   Rebel Pilot A-Wing (2000)   Rebel Pilot A-Wing (2006)   Rebel Pilot A-Wing (2009)   Rebel Pilot A-Wing (2013)   Rebel Pilot B-Wing (2000)   Rebel Pilot B-Wing (2006)

| B-Wing Pilot (2013) | Ten Numb (2006) | Biggs Darklighter (1999) | Dack Ralter (1999) | Dack Ralter (2007) | Jek Porkins (2012) | Wedge Antilles (2006) | Zev Senesca (2010) | Zev Senesca (2011) |

| Rebel Pilot Y-Wing (2004) | Rebel Pilot Y-Wing (2007) | Rebel Pilot Y-Wing (2012) | Snowspeeder Pilot (2013) | Rebel Pilot X-Wing (2012) | X-Wing Fighter Pilot (2014) | Rebel Technician (1999) | Rebel Engineer (2000) | Rebel Technician (2006) |

| Rebel Scout Trooper (2008) | Rebel Scout Trooper (2012) | Hoth Rebel (1999) | Hoth Rebel (2004) | Hoth Rebel (2007) | Hoth Rebel (2009) | Hoth Rebel Trooper (2010) | Hoth Rebel Trooper (2010) | Hoth Rebel Trooper (2012) |

| Hoth Rebel Trooper (2013) | Hoth Officer (2010) | General Rieekan (2013) | Rebel Commando (2009) | Rebel Commando (2009) | Rebel Commando (2012) | Rebel Commando (2012) | Rebel Commando (2013) | Wookiee Warrior (2005) |

| Chewbacca (2004) | Chewbacca (2004) | Chewbacca (2014) | Chief Tarfful (2014) | Lando Calrissian (2003) | Lando Calrissian (2009) | Lando Calrissian (2006) | Lando Calrissian (2012) | Lobot (2002) |

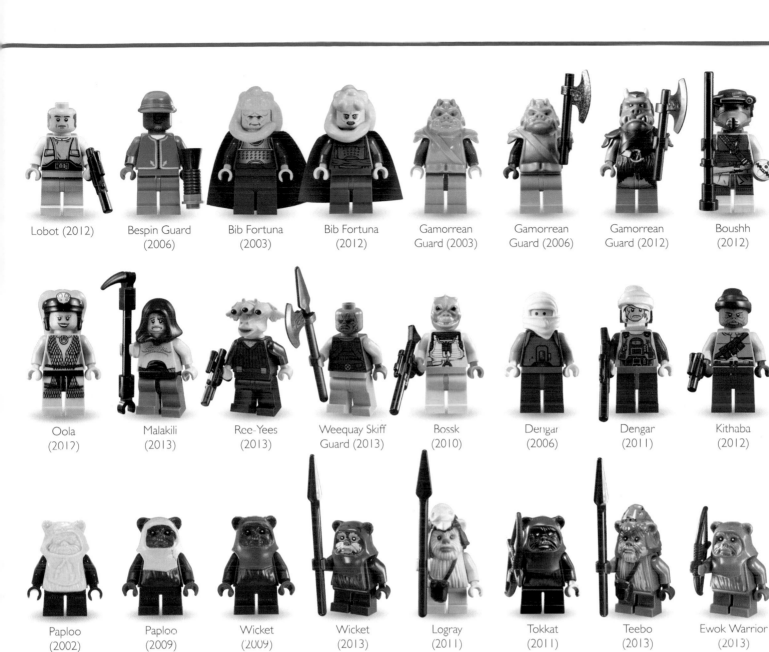

Lobot (2012)

Bespin Guard (2006)

Bib Fortuna (2003)

Bib Fortuna (2012)

Gamorrean Guard (2003)

Gamorrean Guard (2006)

Gamorrean Guard (2012)

Boushh (2012)

Max Rebo (2013)

Oola (2012)

Malakili (2013)

Ree-Yees (2013)

Weequay Skiff Guard (2013)

Bossk (2010)

Dengar (2006)

Dengar (2011)

Kithaba (2012)

Ewok (2002)

Paploo (2002)

Paploo (2009)

Wicket (2009)

Wicket (2013)

Logray (2011)

Tokkat (2011)

Teebo (2013)

Ewok Warrior (2013)

Chief Chirpa (2009)

Darth Malgus (2012)

Darth Vader's Apprentice (2008)

Juno Eclipse (2008)

Jedi Consular (2013)

Jedi Knight (2013)

Shadow Trooper (2007)

Sith Trooper (2012)

Sith Trooper (2013)

Sith Trooper (2013)

Special Forces Clone Trooper (2013)

Separatist Bounty Hunter (2013)

Sith Warrior (2013)

Republic Trooper (2013)

Satele Shan (2012)

Jace Malcom (2012)

T7-O1 (2012)

Jek-14 (2013)

Special Forces Commander (2013)

Set Index

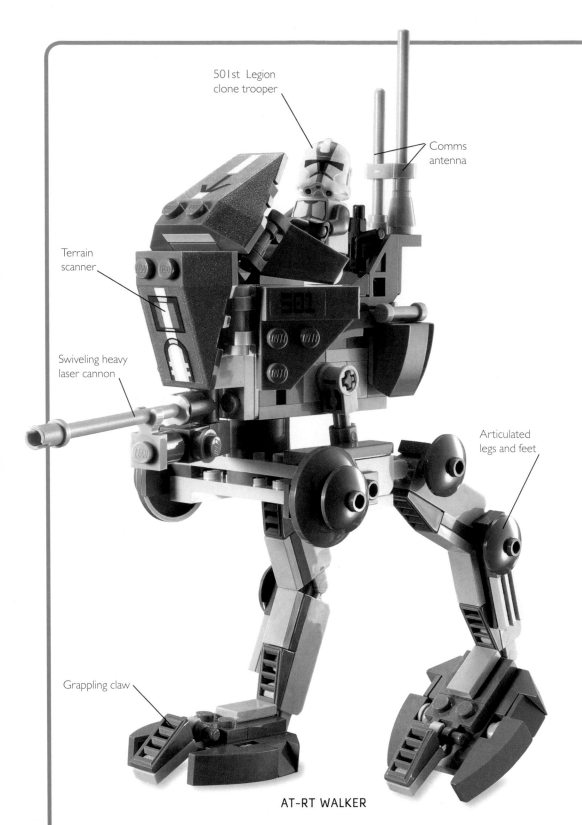

501st Legion
clone trooper

Comms
antenna

Terrain
scanner

Swiveling heavy
laser cannon

Articulated
legs and feet

Grappling claw

AT-RT WALKER

LONDON, NEW YORK, MUNICH,
MELBOURNE, AND DELHI

Senior Editor Sadie Smith
Editors Pamela Afram,
Emma Grange, Kathryn Hill
Designers Jon Hall, Mark Richards,
Thelma-Jane Robb
Pre-Production Producer Siu Yin Chan
Producer Louise Minihane
Managing Editor Elizabeth Dowsett
Design Manager Ron Stobbart
Art Director Lisa Lanzarini
Publishing Manager Julie Ferris
Publishing Director Simon Beecroft

Consultants

Huw Millington and Giles Kemp

First published in the United States in 2009. This updated and
expanded edition published in 2014 by DK Publishing,
345 Hudson Street, New York, New York 10014

10 9 8 7 6 5 4 3 2 1
001-193682-May/14

Discover more at
www.dk.com   www.LEGO.com   www.starwars.com

Acknowledgments

DK would like to thank Randi Kirsten Sørensen,
Luis Gómez, Michael Lee Stockwell, Paul Constantin
Turcanu, Jens Kronvold Frederiksen, Olav Krøigaard,
Kurt Kristiansen, Jan Neergaard Olesen, Mathew
Steven Boyle, Louise Weiss Borup, Lauge Drewes,
and Vibeke Mørk Sørensen at the LEGO Group;
Leland Chee, Jonathan Rinzler, and Carol Roeder
at Lucasfilm; Chelsea Alon at Disney; Nicholas Ricks,
Samuel Delaney, Matthew Ellison, Philip Ring, Tim
Wileman, and Jonathan Smith at TT Games; Ross
Clark at ClicTime and Sun Yu at Zendesign.

The publisher would also like to thank Huw Millington
and Giles Kemp for lending their expert LEGO *Star
Wars* knowledge and the permission to use their
photographs; Gary Ombler for his photography; Jason
Fry and Simon Beecroft for writing; Debra Wolter,
Julia March, and Lauren Nesworthy for proofreading
and editorial help; Suzanne Cooper and Sam Bartlett
for design assistance; Helen Peters for the index.
For his contribution to the first edition of the this
book, DK would like to thank Jeremy Beckett.

PICTURE CREDITS

Images supplied by the LEGO Group. Additional
photography by Gary Ombler, Jeremy Beckett, Sarah
Ashun, and Brian Poulsen. Page 126: Bottom left and
center © Markus Aspacher (markus1984); bottom
right, Han Solo in Carbonite sculpture © Nathan
Sawaya. Photo courtesy of brickartist.com; Page 127:
bottom left © Amado C. Pinlac (ACPin); center right
© Mark Borlase/Brickplumber; bottom right © Je
Hyung Lee (storm TK431); top right © Ian Greig, 2007.